Ready-made assemblies
about famous people

Tony Dobinson

D1331654

Scripture Union

All Bible quotations are from the Good News Bible –
Old Testament: Copyright ©American Bible Society 1976;
New Testament: Copyright ©American Bible Society 1966, 1971,
1976

Every effort has been made to contact all the living subjects for
their approval of the stories. If changes need to be made, we shall
do this in any reprint of the book.

©Tony Dobinson 2000
First published 2000

Scripture Union, 207–209 Queensway, Bletchley, Milton Keynes,
MK2 2EB, England

ISBN 1 85999 300 1

British Library Cataloguing-in-Publication Data.
A catalogue record of this book is available from the British
Library.

Printed and bound in Great Britain by
Stanley L. Hunt (Printers) Ltd., Rushden, Northamptonshire.

CONTENTS

SECTION THREE: JUSTICE
Stories of those who suffered injustice and those who strove
to help them.

SECTION FOUR: HOPE
Stories of those who put their trust in God and found their
hope was not in vain.

SECTION FIVE: FORGIVENESS
Stories of those whose understanding of God's forgiveness shaped their response to others.

FOREWORD

People matter to people especially in our post-modern culture. Institutions have lost their appeal, even though issues have not. That is why this book will be a winner with its intended audience as they encounter significant people from the past and the present.

The genius of Tony Dobinson's approach is that campaign issues are also explored; bullying and racism find a place alongside forgiveness for murderers and the slave trade.

But it will also be a success with its users. There is just the right detail together with some great ideas to draw the listeners into active encounter with the people they hear about.

The book has another brilliant touch. Its main sections follow The Open Book issues of Identity, Freedom, Justice, Hope and Forgiveness. We know these are vitally important today, but what is more they link to a whole range of Open Book resources which can be used to explore these themes with young people when the opportunities arise.

This book will be a welcome resource not only for those taking school assemblies but also for churches wanting to challenge the causes of indifference to the Bible in their own communities.

David Spriggs, The Project Director,
The Open Book, Bible Society.

ABOUT THIS BOOK

"Oh, Mr Carter..."

"Yes, Headmaster?"

"Would you be able to take this morning's assembly for me? I've got a parent who's just come in..."

"Oh. Right. Yes."

"It starts in ten minutes, all right?"

"Err... right, Headmaster."

"Oh, Mr Carter, before you run off, if it could link in with Year Four's topic on Africa, that would be good."

"Err... right, Headmaster."

"And the head of Year Six wanted me to do something on bullying, I seem to remember."

"Err..."

"Well, I'll just leave it to you then, Mr Carter."

"Err... thanks, Headmaster."

Exaggerated perhaps (at least I hope so) but all of us who take school assemblies have faced the problem: finding just the right material with the minimum of fuss and time.

This book offers an answer – in fact twenty-four answers in the form of twenty-four stories from the lives of famous people. All the material you need to make the stories relevant to juniors is included between these covers. But I hope this book will do more than make life easy for you: I hope that through the stories of these men and women of God the children will come to see God as real, reachable and interested in their lives. The assemblies are grouped in five sections – Creation and Identity, Freedom, Justice, Hope, Forgiveness. Some of the assemblies may be considered more suitable for the upper end of the age range.

The basic format for each assembly is the same, comprising the following sections:

THE PROBLEM

describes a fictional situation involving children, usually ending with the main character having to make a difficult decision.

It is followed by questions to get the listeners thinking through the options. These can be used for discussion if you wish.

(N.B. Be sensitive to your audience: in some cases embarrassment and hurt could be caused if the situation is too close to that of a particular child, or if the name of a character makes the listeners think you are getting at a child with the same name.)

THE STORY

is a true story about a famous person, focusing on a time when that person was in a similar situation to the child in THE PROBLEM and showing how their Christian beliefs guided them in dealing with it.

TIME OF REFLECTION

is to help children see the relevance of THE STORY to their own lives.

BIBLE BITS

gives Bible verses appropriate to the theme.

PRAYER

suggests a short, informal prayer relevant to what's gone before.

This basic material, without a discussion time, will take about ten minutes, perhaps a little more, to read aloud. If you have short assemblies then you could use THE PROBLEM and the discussion pointers on one occasion, the rest on the next. If however you want a longer assembly and have more time to prepare than Mr Carter, then you may wish to use the following:

VARIATIONS ON A THEME

offers suggestions for involving the children through drama etc.

QUIZ QUESTIONS

gives ten factual questions on THE STORY. This section does not appear for all assemblies – in some cases the natural light-heartedness of a quiz would work against the serious mood the assembly has tried to establish. There are some ideas for quiz formats at the end of the book.

A teacher who trialled some of the assemblies found it worked to stop reading THE STORY at certain points and say, "Now talk with the person next to you about what you think happens next", or "How would you feel if this happened to you?"

So – how would Mr Carter find the right assembly? He would use the SUBJECTLINK index at the back of the book and find – Phew! – that the story about Mary Slessor would bring in Africa and bullying as requested. The contents page gives you a more general idea of what the stories are about.

I have tried to make the book as teacher-friendly and as "instant" as possible, but obviously it is best if you have the time to read through the whole assembly before using it, to decide which sections to use, alter any wording which won't roll off your particular tongue, make the prayer more relevant to the situation in your school, and so on.

What? They're lining up for assembly already ...?

MOTHER TERESA

Caring about the poor – social work in India

Other themes: respect for the homeless, peer pressure

THE PROBLEM

Listen to this story and see what you think at the end.

"Shhh!" whispered Tim. "Don't wake up Sleeping Beauty over there!"

Adam and Paul looked across at the park bench. A shabbily dressed figure was lying on it, one arm under his head, both feet up on the bench and displaying very holey socks. His shoes were under the bench, side by side.

"It's old Fred," murmured Paul.

"Yeah," said Tim. "The one and only Filthy Fred."

Adam wasn't sure they should call Fred that, but he knew his mates meant no harm. They often saw Fred on their way home from school. He'd be shuffling along the road, or just gazing into shop windows. Adam had been told he was harmless, that he'd just had such an unhappy, disturbed childhood and that he'd never been able to settle into a home or a job.

"Let's play catch," said Tim.

He crept over to the bench and picked up one of Fred's shoes between two fingers.

"Urgh!" he shouted, grinning. "I don't want this. You have it." And he threw it to Paul.

Paul shrieked. "Urgh, no thanks. It's horrible. It might bite."

And back and forth the shoe went.

Fred had woken up by now and was sitting upright. To Adam,

11

he looked miserable and confused.

Then Adam heard, "Here, you have it." And the shoe fell at his feet.

He picked it up, thought for a moment, "Maybe I should give it back." But Tim would think that was daft, and anyway, it was only Fred, not anyone important.

Now think:
Is it true that Fred is "not anyone important"? What do you think Fred's feelings are as he sees his shoe being thrown around? Should Adam give it back?

(You could discuss this or pass on to the main story.)

THE STORY

This is the true story of someone who believed the poor are very important. She became famous all over the world, but few would recognize her real name: Agnes Gonxha Bojaxhiu.

Agnes was born on August 26th, 1910. Her parents were from Albania in southern Europe, but the family now lived in Serbia. Even as a child, Agnes cared for the sick and elderly, visiting them with her mother. She also enjoyed writing poetry and playing the mandolin – and she loved praying. Talking to God and sharing what she had – these were the things which made her happiest.

So perhaps it's not surprising that she became a nun. She felt God wanted her to join a particular group – the Catholic Loreto nuns who work in northern India.

So when she was 18, she took on a new name, Sister Teresa, and travelled out to Calcutta, one of India's most crowded cities. She was to live in the convent with its high walls and shady gardens and spend some of her time teaching in the High School in the convent grounds.

But she was also to teach in a little school in the slums.

Nothing had prepared her for what she saw there. It was a different world. She saw people who were starving right there on the streets, looking like little bundles of bones wrapped up in skin. She saw beggars stumbling on legs like long dead twigs, their arms stretched out for help. She saw mothers slouched in doorways, rocking babies too sick or too hungry to cry. She saw people digging into dustbins for food scraps, anything which could be sucked or chewed to keep them going for another day.

But she saw something else too. In the slum school she saw how the faces of the children changed when she smiled at them. She would get the smile back a hundredfold. The children seemed to come to life when they realised someone cared. You see, they were hungry not just for food, but for smiles, for hugs, for love.

The years went by, and Teresa prayed more and more for the people of the slums.

And one day God spoke to her: "You are to leave the convent, Teresa. You are to go out to the poor. You are to live amongst them and care for them."

This would be a new thing in Calcutta. Many people worked with the poor, but the poor always had to come to them for help – to the hospitals, the schools, and so on. But Teresa was to work in the slums themselves.

It was not easy to get permission to leave the convent.

"Are you sure this is what God wants?" they said.

"It's too dangerous for a woman by herself," they said.

"Why not wait?" they said.

Teresa knew they meant it for the best, but she had made her decision. The poor people were on God's heart, and they were on hers too.

After a long wait permission came, and on August 16th 1948, she changed from her nun's clothes to the simple sari which Indian women wear, and walked out of the convent gates. She had just a little money and a train ticket to a town called Patna, where there was a hospital willing to train her in basic nursing.

Soon she was back in Calcutta, in one of the worst slum areas, Motijhil.

She sat in a little square, picked up a stick and began to write letters and numbers in the mud. Children gathered round. Teresa's school had begun! But this was a special school, for Teresa also wanted to teach them how to keep clean, how to avoid disease.

Then she thought: But words are not enough. They need

practical help and they need it now. So she called on people she knew and pleaded: "I need soap. And food. And medicines." She gave away all she collected. And she always remembered to give that something which costs nothing – a smile. The slum children and their families saw not just soap and food and medicine, but they saw love in her smiling eyes.

For Teresa was determined to treat each of them as if they were Jesus himself. So she didn't turn away when a dying man showed her his wounds crawling with maggots. She dressed the wounds, then sat there giving him comfort, despite the appalling smell. Each person was precious to her. She could see Jesus in each one.

Other nuns saw what she was doing and joined her. The city officials let them have an unused building which they turned into a hospice for dying people, a place where they could pass from this world with someone holding their hand.

The nuns became known as the Missionaries of Charity, with Teresa as their leader, their "mother". And that is the name by which Agnes became known – Mother Teresa.

Later in her life she met with presidents and prime ministers to plead for the rights of the poor, but whether the people she met were powerful or down-and-out, rich or poor, she kept on giving the kind word, the loving look, the gentle smile. Right up till she died in 1997.

TIME OF REFLECTION

Let's think about our attitude: when we see the poor, the homeless – or just those who can't do what we do, who don't have what we have – do we look down on them, poke fun at them, think them less important?

Just a moment's silence then, so we can think about how we treat people less fortunate than ourselves.

BIBLE BITS

Jesus said, "I was hungry and you fed me, thirsty and you gave me a drink... I was sick and you took care of me..." For, "whenever you did this for one of the least important of these brothers of mine, you did it for me."   (Matthew 25)

And he said, "There is more happiness in giving than in receiving."

(Acts 20:35)

The Bible also tells us: "You must never treat people in different ways according to their outward appearance."

(James 2:1)

PRAYER

Help us, Father God, never ever to look down on another human being. Help us to realise that every single person is special to you. Amen

VARIATIONS ON A THEME

THE PROBLEM story can be acted out by pupils.

Or if there is a project for the poor in your own area, it would be good to mention it – or maybe more than mention it, maybe collect for it. Enquire first about the needs – blankets, tinned food or whatever.

QUIZ QUESTIONS

1. What made Agnes (or Teresa) happiest when she was young?
2. How old was she when she went to India?
3. What was the difference between the two schools she taught in?
4. Why did she go to Patna?
5. How did she begin her own school in the slums?
6. She pleaded for three things – one was soap. Tell me one more.
7. And the third?
8. She treated each poor person as if he were – who?
9. One thing she gave cost nothing to give – what was it?
10. Why did she meet with presidents and prime ministers?

JOHN HARPER

Caring about those in danger – the Titanic disaster

Other themes: sacrifice, generosity, Easter

THE PROBLEM

Listen to this. What would you do in this situation?

Colin wasn't surprised when it happened. His best mate Billy had been looking pale since lunch. So as soon as Billy put his hands to his mouth Colin was shouting down the coach, "Mrs James, Billy's being sick."

Mrs James got there with the sickbag just in time. Colin watched it fill up with a mixture of horror and relief. What a time for it to happen though, he thought, Billy's going to miss the fun. It was the last night of the residential school trip and they were going to a big fun pool with flumes and chutes. It'd be great, surrounded by their mates – Colin couldn't wait to show off a bit.

He saw Mrs James in the hostel corridor after tea. "Is he okay now?"

"Far from it, I'm afraid. Good for him we're going home tomorrow. Oh, Colin, he's asked if you could stay with him this evening. He said your awful jokes were the only things that would cheer him up."

"But... it's the swimming tonight."

"Yes, it's a sacrifice, I know. Anyway, think about it. There'll be a couple of teachers here, so don't feel you have to."

Then she smiled and turned away, leaving Colin biting his lip in the corridor.

Now think:
What should Colin do? What if he stays back and Billy just falls asleep? But they are best friends...

(You could discuss this or pass on to the main story.)

THE STORY

It's hard to give something up. But I want to tell you about someone who gave up far more than one evening, and for someone he didn't even know.

As they reached the bottom of the ship's gangway, it would be impossible to say who was the more excited – John Harper or his six-year-old daughter, Nan – for neither of them had experienced anything like this. They were about to board the largest, the most luxurious ship ever built, the ship everyone had been talking about. It was the first one with a swimming pool, and there were Turkish baths, even four-poster beds on board – and fantastic meals to look forward to.

John Harper was a church minister from Scotland. He'd now been invited to preach in the States. And this marvellous ship was sailing to New York on just the right day. What an opportunity!

But the great thing about this ship was its safety – the hull was divided into sixteen watertight compartments. If there was a collision the worst that could happen was that one compartment, or two at the most, would be cracked open. But the ship could still float if four were smashed. In fact, the ship was nicknamed "The Unsinkable". Its real name was impressive too – it meant mighty and enormous. It was called... the *Titanic*.

Midday, April 10th, 1912. The tugs began pulling the ship away from Southampton docks. Soon, under its own steam, the *Titanic* was surging majestically towards the open sea. The great adventure had begun!

What no-one on board knew was that a huge chain of icebergs was lying across their path to New York. And only a few officers knew two other facts – that the binoculars used for spotting icebergs had gone missing from the crow's nest, the lookout point, and that there were only enough lifeboats for one thousand two hundred people. There were over *two* thousand two hundred on board.

John and Nan were having a wonderful time. John had always

enjoyed the water, even though he had come close to drowning not once, not twice, but three times: first when he fell down a well when he was two – his mother had to hold him upside down while the water poured out; then in his twenties: while taking a dip a strong current almost dragged him out to sea; then in his thirties a boat he was on sprung a leak. Perhaps these events were to prepare him for what was to come.

John had become a Christian when he was thirteen by hearing a Bible verse, John 3:16 – perhaps you know it – "God loved the world so much that he gave his only son". So John understood straightaway that the Christian life was about giving – God gave, now he should give. And he did, giving time, energy and love to the poor and needy around Glasgow. He became a famous preacher too.

He had been to America before, but not with Nan. They were over halfway there now.

Almost midnight on April 14th. The men in the crow's nest were finding it difficult to see. There was no moon and the binoculars had not been found. There – was that an iceberg ahead? Yes! "Hard a' starboard!" Yes... yes, just made it. Lumps of ice fell on the decks as the ship brushed past. Phew! That was a close one! Then came a crunching, grinding sound from below. The ship seemed to be trembling as if in fear or pain. For ten seconds, that was all.

But in those ten seconds the part of the iceberg they couldn't see had smashed open six of the watertight compartments.

Six.

More than two. More than four.

The *Titanic* was doomed.

There came a knock on John's cabin door, on every door. "Put your life-jackets on. Go to Boat Deck." When he and Nan got there, he saw the crew hurrying to take the covers off the lifeboats. Then the boats were lowered and the cry went out: "Women and children first!" John hugged his daughter and made sure she got into a lifeboat. Nan did not know that was the last time she would see her father.

Now the third class passengers, with much further to come, began crowding onto the deck. And then the panic began. People could see the *Titanic* was going down quickly, could see that there weren't enough lifeboats for them all.

John saw that many of them did not even have a life-jacket. He knew what God wanted him to do. He took off his own and gave it to a stranger. He knew he was probably giving his life as well.

Waves were washing over the deck now and the ship was tilting more and more. John had no choice. Like many others, he clambered onto the railings and dropped into the freezing sea.

As he entered the water perhaps he remembered the three times he had been rescued from drowning. But he knew this was different. Around him he could hear screams, cries of despair. And he thought, Do they know about heaven? He began calling out, "Believe on the Lord Jesus and you will be safe for ever." A man desperately clinging to a piece of wreckage heard those words and remembered them. John went on shouting out the same words. Until the cold overpowered him and he slipped beneath the waves.

1502 people died that night. But that man clinging to the wreckage was picked up by a rescue boat and later told how he had become a Christian through John's last words.

And Nan? She was rescued, returned to Scotland and eventually married a church minister.

But what about the person to whom John gave his life-jacket – and his life? We've no idea. But John knew that he was doing what God wanted him to do, and for him that would have been enough.

TIME OF REFLECTION

Think now. God wants us to be not just takers but givers too. Probably we won't be asked to give our life for someone, but would we be willing to give an afternoon or an evening, to help someone, to cheer someone up? Or perhaps we own something that someone else needs more than us. Are we givers or just takers? Let's think about ourselves for a moment...

Now let's think of those who've given so much to us, families, friends, strangers.

BIBLE BITS

Listen to what the Bible says:

"Look out for one another's interests, not just for your own. The attitude you should have is the one that Jesus Christ had."

(Philippians 2:4,5)

"Be generous and ready to share with others."

(1 Timothy 6:18)

PRAYER

Thank you, Jesus, that you gave your life. You could have called on angels to get you down from the cross, but you didn't. Thank you for John Harper. And thank you for those who have seen what we need and have given it to us. Help us to appreciate more, and to give more. Amen

VARIATIONS ON A THEME

At some point near the end of the assembly, it could be effective if several pupils told of times when someone gave up something for them. Aim for a wide range of "sacrifices" – the mundane to the vitally important, and a wide range of "givers" too – not just the children's best friends.

Alternatively, if the time is right, the Harper story could lead into the story of the crucifixion and the events leading up to it. The episode of Jesus praying in Gethsemane brings out the idea of willingness no matter what the cost.

CHRISTIAN SPORTSPEOPLE:
Cyrille Regis, Chris Powell, Va'aiga Tuigamala, Judy Simpson

Caring about the team – football, rugby, etc.

Other themes: valuing and supporting others, working together

THE PROBLEM

Listen to this and see what you think.

"Right, class," said Mr Barnes, "let me remind you what to do: in your groups, you have to produce a realistic front page of a newspaper, making up the news, adverts and so on. I want to see everyone busy. You've only got until lunch, so don't waste time. The best one will be put on display for parents' evening."

Sophie cast an eye over her team and sighed. "Look," she said, "let's be honest – you know I'm the best writer and the best artist in this group, so why don't you all read or something and let me get on with it?"

"But we want to take part," said Ricky. "And I can write a sports report better than you."

"Sports? On the front page?" Sophie sneered. "Look, we want to win, don't we?"

"Yeah," mumbled Ricky, "guess so."

Anne-Marie in the next group was listening to the conversation. She knew she was just as talented as Sophie, and certainly the best writer and artist in her group.

And she wanted her group to win. So should she, like Sophie, just do it all herself? Or was there, she wondered, a better way?

Now think:
Is there a better way? Do you think Sophie's group would enjoy the morning – or learn much? What would be the advantages in sharing out the work?

(You could discuss this or pass on to the main story.)

THE STORY

It was almost too good to be true. Coventry City had reached the 1987 FA Cup Final. After years of struggling to keep their place in the ratings, here they were in the final! Of course they wouldn't win, no chance of that against Tottenham Hotspur. Spurs had won the cup more than once already, against top teams too. And they had star players; Coventry had... err... well...

But they would give it a go. They could only come second.

The start couldn't have been worse. Spurs scored in the first two minutes. The Coventry fans must have wondered what the final score would be. At this rate... it didn't bear thinking about.

But then something happened. Coventry started playing more as a team, supporting each other, encouraging each other. This came naturally to them as they were all friends off the pitch, used to laughing and joking together. The team spirit was really strong.

And they equalised. One all now.

But could they keep it up? Yes, they certainly could. It was two all when they went into extra time. Unbelievable!

The teams were tired now. But each member of the Coventry team wanted to carry on giving 100%. No one wanted to let his team-mates down. So they ran hard for each other, gave each other a bit of a boost when it was needed. And the final result? Three – two to Coventry!

The star players had lost. The team players had won.

It had taken a lot of courage and determination to keep going like that. But at least one of the Coventry players was very used to showing those qualities. Cyrille Regis had always been a fighter. For a start, he's black, and when he came into top class professional football in the seventies, there were very few black players. When he went out on the pitch, there'd be lots of racial abuse – name-calling and booing. But he knew he couldn't let it get to him, that would be letting the team down. He just had to prove to the crowd how well a black footballer could play and win their respect that way.

And he needed courage too when he became a Christian. It wasn't easy to tell his mates that he was following Jesus now, and that had become the most important thing. Perhaps his mates thought he wouldn't give 100% to the game any more. But it wasn't like that. He began playing with a new energy, a new enjoyment. He'd realised his talent came from God himself, so he wasn't going to start wasting it. Anyway he knew God wouldn't want him to let his team down.

Now after twenty years as a player, Cyrille has gone into coaching. He doesn't yell and swear at the team to get the best out of them. He knows if Jesus were the coach, he wouldn't be swearing and getting angry. And Jesus knew how to get the best out of his team all right. We know one left the team – Judas – but the eleven who stayed on made quite a side!

One player who's been a fan of Cyrille's for years is Chris Powell who played for Derby County before moving to Charlton Athletic. Chris is also black – his parents are Jamaican – and he admires the way Cyrille just went out there and won respect for black players. Chris aims to have that same good attitude.

It's not always easy. He knows if a match is being televised, any tiny mistake, any show of frustration or anger is really going to show. And if he's fouled or the referee makes a decision against him, Chris's reaction might be seen by millions of people.

But, like Cyrille, Chris is a Christian and that means he can pray about each game, and he knows Jesus is alongside him, ready to steady him and make him able to accept decisions even if he believes they're wrong.

And if it *is* his fault – and nobody's perfect – then he knows it's no good letting it spoil the game, God wouldn't want that. Just say sorry where it's needed and get on.

It's no wonder then that Chris enjoys his football. He always has – from the time he played for Crystal Palace as a schoolboy, through his time with Southend United and then with Derby. He prayed about each of these moves, for he believes that it's not where he can get the most money or fame that counts, but where God wants him. He's always wanted to play for Spurs, but that wasn't on God's list!

What made him so happy at Derby was the team spirit. There was a good manager and supportive team-mates, and these things are really important. You've got to want to give 100% for each other.

And not just in football – Va'aiga Tuigamala, who plays Rugby Union for Newcastle, says the same. In one vital game he injured his knee, the pain was terrible. When it had happened before like this, he'd been unable to move. This was the worst time for it to happen again, his team-mates were depending on him. So he prayed, really quickly – what some people call an arrow prayer – and, yes, he could move, he could run, and he carried on running – even into extra time!

But he knows the prayer worked because it was part of an ongoing friendship with Jesus, a God who cared about him and about his role in that team.

Being in a team demands a lot, but it gives a lot too. Judy Simpson is an Olympic athlete used to battling solo. Then she joined the Gladiators TV programme, and her favourite game on it was Powerball – because for once she was in a team, she could feel the support teamwork can give.

All these sportspeople are Christians, so they're not only in their sports teams, they're in Jesus' team as well. Being in his team is very demanding too, but at least they know they've got a great manager who isn't going to resign, or throw them out of the team – ever!

TIME OF REFLECTION

It's not easy to be a good team player – it means you're there for the team, not just for yourself. Jesus showed what that could mean – losing sleep when his team needed him, serving his team rather than bossing them about, giving 100% even when he was worn out.

When you're in a team, doing group work or playing a sport, are you a good person to have around?

Just take a moment to think about that.

BIBLE BITS

Teamwork is good for us. The Bible says:

"People learn from one another, just as iron sharpens iron."
(Proverbs 27:17)

But we need to play our part. It also says:

"Depending on an unreliable person ... is like trying to chew with a loose tooth."
(Proverbs 25:19)

So be like iron, not like a loose tooth!

PRAYER

Lord, when I'm in a group or team, whether it's in the class-room, or on the sports field, or in the gym, or anywhere, help me to respect and value my team-mates, and help me to give 100% to the team. Thank you that you gave 100% because you value us so much. Amen

VARIATIONS ON A THEME

Pupils could talk about when they've been in groups or teams and have been supported or encouraged by a team-mate or mates.

Or you could think about teams in the Bible – Jesus' team, as in THE STORY, or Paul's team, or David's team (see 2 Samuel 23:8 onwards).

QUIZ QUESTIONS

1. Which teams played in the 1987 FA Cup Final?
2. What was the final score?
3. What did Coventry do to win?
4. How did Cyrille Regis show courage?
5. And when he – ?
6. What did he do after twenty years of playing football?
7. Where are Chris Powell's parents from?
8. Which team did he play for as a schoolboy?
9. Why was he happy at Derby?
10. Why did Va'aiga Tuigamala's prayer work so well?

JOSIAH SPIERS

Caring about children – the beginnings of Scripture Union

Other themes: prayer, the friendship of Jesus

THE PROBLEM

Listen to this and see what you think.

The assembly was over and the children began returning to their classrooms. Liam had enjoyed the story that morning – about how there'd been this great storm on the lake and how the disciples in their little fishing boat saw that Jesus had dozed off and shouted out to him, "Don't you care about us?" and how Jesus proved he cared by standing up in the boat and stopping the storm.

After the story the Headteacher had prayed, "Thank you, Lord, that you still care about us."

That made Liam think. Did Jesus care? It mattered to him because the situation at home was, well, rather stormy, and sometimes he felt that no one cared about him.

"Hey, Scott," he began as they settled back into their class places. "Do you think God cares about people today? I mean, like, would he listen if... I prayed?"

Scott shrugged. "Don't think so, no. Like I mean, he's got his hands full with important stuff. He's got to listen to everyone in the world, hasn't he? He's bound to listen to archbishops and prime ministers first. And all those who know the proper words. And he's got to keep the earth turning, and stop meteors crashing into it, and deal with earthquakes and forest fires and... well, doesn't leave much time for us, does it?"

"No," said Liam sighing. "Guess not."

Now think:

Is God too busy to care about Liam? Would he listen to him or has he got more important people to think about?

(You could discuss this or pass on to the main story.)

THE STORY

We're going back about 150 years to Queen Victoria's time and we're sitting in church. So sit up straight – you're in your very best clothes and definitely on your best behaviour. Though in fact you probably wouldn't be sitting down here in the main congregation – you'd be up in the gallery. You see, it was thought by many well-off people that God and the Bible were for adults only, so you'd be pushed up there and told to be quiet while your parents listened to a l-o-o-ong sermon, maybe lasting an hour and in very difficult language, and sing l-o-o-ong solemn hymns.

You could look down on them from up there. There they'd be – the men all waistcoats and whiskers, the ladies all bonnets and bows. And all sitting very, very still.

If you were up in the gallery, what would you be thinking about?

(You can ask for a response or just give the ideas here.)

"When's it going to end?", or, "I'm dying to stretch, or sneeze, or y-a-a-awn, or go to the toilet", or maybe, "God must be a very boring person."

Now let's go to another church, in the centre of London – there's something very unusual happening here. An American called Payson Hammond has advertised a service especially for children. For children!

It's very different. The children, over a thousand of them, are sitting in the main part of the church – the adults are stuck up in the gallery! – the songs are lively and the words Mr Hammond uses are easy to understand. There are even jokes!

Even the adults are enjoying it! Look, there's one, Josiah Spiers he's called, as bright-eyed and attentive as any of the children.

And later, at home, that man got to thinking. Thinking: yes, that's how it should be – children enjoying church. But he was thinking too about the fact that the preacher had asked the children if they wanted to be God's friend, if they wanted to get to know him personally. A child? Unheard of up to then. An adult, yes, when they'd learnt enough long religious words so they could talk to God "properly", but – a child?

But, thought Josiah, why not? Hadn't Jesus been angry with his disciples when they'd tried to keep children away? "Let the children come to me," he'd said. Surely then, God cared about children, listened to their prayers. Why, Jesus had even told people off for praying long, fancy prayers full of religious words. He seemed to want people to pray like children.

Josiah told his artist friend, Thomas Hughes, about the children's service.

"Well," said Thomas, "we've got a big sitting room, so we can have a similar service for the local kids here. Shall we try it? You'll speak and lead the singing, Josiah, won't you?"

"Err..." Josiah hesitated. He was a little chap, rather shy, an office worker, not used to things like this. But – he'd have a go.

Fifteen children came. Josiah began a story about Jesus and soon forgot his shyness.

It was a brilliant success. Josiah must have thought, "I didn't know I could do that." But he had done that and he did it again the next week when many more children came. Then one weekly meeting wasn't enough, so they had a Wednesday one as well. Then the Hughes' sitting room wasn't large enough, so they hired a schoolroom. Hundreds of children were coming now. Phew!

After a year Josiah needed a holiday. Could he afford it? – normally only the better off had holidays... Yes, he could. Now where? Let's see... Llandudno, North Wales. Nice, restful spot.

Ah, this is pleasant. Josiah breathed in the clean air and surveyed the beach. Adults were sitting on hard chairs, talking, the men still in their waistcoats, the women still in their bonnets and bows. Some children, also fully clothed apart from shoes and socks, were playing a little game nearby. As Josiah watched, he realised – these are the children from wealthy families who would never be allowed to go to a children's meeting or a Sunday School, these are the gallery children, the ones who probably believe God's a bore.

And he couldn't resist it. Before he'd thought of his nerves, he'd gathered them round and begun a story about Jesus. The sun didn't stop him dancing about, doing all the voices, making a show of it. The children loved it – more, more!

So Josiah gave them more.

Tomorrow, tomorrow, they shouted.

Well, err, yes, why not, thought Josiah. It's not exactly a rest, but why not? He added in songs and games – he was a great rounders player, by the way.

By the end of the week several hundred children were gathering on the beach to hear him. The parents were delighted. And so the invitations started.

"Err, Mr Spiers, would you be prepared to come to our town and do something similar on our beach?"

"Oh Mr Spiers, can you come to our village? We don't have a beach, but we have a large village green and very well-behaved children, I promise."

And just at this time, Josiah was left some money – by a man who'd run a waistcoat factory – and you know how popular waistcoats were! So he gave up his job and accepted the invitations. And those gallery children came in their hundreds to listen to his stories, sing his catchy songs, and learn about a God who cared as much for a child as he did for an archbishop.

Often over a thousand children would come to a meeting, and there was never a discipline problem – or a yawning problem! He would have made a terrific schoolteacher.

And did the children find the message was true or just words? Josiah knew from the many letters children wrote to him that Jesus could become as real to them as he was to Josiah himself. They could know his friendship and love for themselves.

Many people joined Josiah, it became quite an organisation. Some of them even went abroad. And the organisation is still going today. It's called Scripture Union. They still run holidays and beach missions for children as well as publishing lots of children's books – including... that's right – this one!

TIME OF REFLECTION

Let's think for a moment. Perhaps you believe in God strongly, perhaps just a bit, but – do you believe he really cares for you, that he's really interested in you? If you believed that, what difference would it make?

BIBLE BITS

Jesus said: "Let the children come to me, and do not stop them, because the Kingdom of God belongs to such as these."

(Mark 10:14)

"Leave all your worries with him, because he cares for you."

(I Peter 5:7)

PRAYER

Thank you for people like Josiah Spiers who made services fun and interesting so younger people could understand about you. Thank you for the teachers in this school who make learning interesting. And to repeat that Head's prayer in the first story – thank you, Lord, that you still care about us. Amen

VARIATION ON A THEME

Two groups of children could act out short scenes showing the two kinds of service mentioned in the story: child-oriented and adult-oriented.

QUIZ QUESTIONS

1. Who was on the throne in Josiah Spiers' time?
2. Name one surprise Josiah had at the special children's service.
3. And another.
4. Why did Jesus get angry with his disciples?
5. How many children came to the first service in the Hughes' sitting room?
6. Why did Josiah not want to speak at the meeting?
7. Where did he go on holiday?
8. Why was he so keen to tell the beach children that God was not boring?
9. What game could he play well?
10. What is the present name of the organisation he started?

THOMAS ARMITAGE

Caring about the disabled – the Royal National Institute for the Blind

Other themes: thinking positively, using our talents

THE PROBLEM

Listen to this story: there's something to think about at the end.

Robbie hated school sports day. Worst day of the year, he reckoned. For Robbie couldn't run; he'd probably never be able to. He could walk a bit, but if he tried to run, he'd fall flat on his face. And as they didn't have a falling over event, that was that, he couldn't take part.

So he just sat with his house, the Swallows, and watched as his mates were called up to the starting line, and as they came back with bits of coloured ribbon pinned to their shirts. He felt a right nerd, for what could he do for his house? Nothing. Everyone understood but that wasn't the point.

The gun went for the start of the 400 metres. His best friend, Joe Collins, was in this for the Swallows. Not that he'd win, but Robbie would give him a cheer as he got to the finish, hopefully not too far behind the others.

But what was this? Joe for the first time was keeping up, arms and legs pumping away. Robbie had never seen him like this before.

And, look, he's up to second place now, just behind Matthew Drew.

He's coming up level!

Robbie could see Joe's face, bursting with effort. Without thinking, he pushed himself up from his seat and started yelling, "Go on, Joe! Go on! You can do it!"

He was vaguely aware of faces turning to look at him for a second. "Go on, Joe!" he screamed.

Still level, only a few yards to go.

And Robbie was waving his arms wildly, calling out Joe's name. "Joe! Joe!"

Suddenly it was over. Who'd won? They'd seemed level at the tape.

And then Robbie saw. There he was, his best mate Joe with the gold ribbon for first, striding back to his house like a king.

"Great stuff, Joe," Robbie grinned at him. "Knew you could do it."

Joe grinned back. "Couldn't have done it without you though, Robbie. It was your shouting that did it. I could hear you above everything. Thanks, mate."

A few minutes later, Mr Broomfield, the teacher in charge of Swallows house, came up to Robbie and said, "Come on, lad, with a voice like that, I'm making you official cheerleader for the Swallows tug-of-war team."

So, as the team grabbed the rope, a chair was put for Robbie close by. Given official permission to make a noise, Robbie made the most of it. "Pull, I said, pull... and pull, get up, James, pull!"

And suddenly the Swallows fell backwards. They'd won.

"Well done, Robbie," said Mr Broomfield later. "You've got a voice and a half there."

"Yeah, but..." Robbie began. "That's all I can do – shout. I can't take part."

Now think:
Did Robbie take part that day? Did he let his house down because he couldn't run?

(You could discuss this or pass on to the main story.)

THE STORY

Now for a true story. It starts in the year 1860.

It was no use. He'd have to give up.

The one thing he wanted to do in life, to help others through medicine, he would no longer be able to do. For he was going blind.

So, he thought, what now?

Yes, he thought, *what?* I have great knowledge, and I can't use it. I have the desire to help people get better, but I can't help them. I am wealthy enough to give treatment to those who can't pay, but I can't see to give them treatment. I can't, I can't, I can't...

Thomas Armitage had had trouble with his sight before when he was a medical student. His eyes had not been able to cope with the amount of reading he had to do. So he had taken a long rest and eventually he'd been able to go on with his studies, becoming a qualified doctor and surgeon. But the trouble was more severe now. A rest would not help him this time.

He prayed into the stillness. "Lord, you understand. You know all I wanted to do for people, for you. And now – I can't. Oh, Lord – what use can I be if I'm blind?"

But then an idea began to grow in his mind... For, yes, there was something he could do, a group of people he perhaps could help, people whose problems he'd be able to understand very well now.

Blind people.

They certainly needed help, he knew that. For it was difficult for blind people to get jobs, and if they had no family willing and able to care for them, then they had to beg. It could be a desperately sad life.

And he realised what would change all this: if they could be taught to read. Some could already, by running their fingers over raised type or patterns which represented the different letters of the alphabet. But there were so many systems, so many types of type! So a blind person could only read what was produced in the system he knew.

What was needed was for everything to be produced in one system. But who should decide which? It was obvious to Thomas Armitage. Blind people should decide.

So he brought together a little group of blind men to examine every system of reading by touch that they could lay their hands on, if you'll excuse the joke. Not just British ones but foreign ones too.

Many other people were asked for their opinions as they went along – many blind people, that is.

Eventually one system came out tops – the one devised by a French lad called Louis Braille when he was just fifteen. It used different patterns of up to six raised dots to represent each letter, number and so on.

Through Dr Armitage's efforts more and more was printed in the Braille system, with the doctor taking a personal interest in everything to make sure what was produced was the best. He was doing this work for God.

So it was his fingers that checked each hill and valley on the Braille maps, and when sheets of Braille print were stamped out, he would take them home for varnishing in his own kitchen, where they were hung up to dry amongst all the pots and pans. Fortunately his wife was as keen as he was, so she didn't mind.

And so a whole world of reading was opened up to blind people, as not only books and maps were published in Braille, but also music scores and, I'm afraid, exam papers, and even, would you believe it, times tables. No excuse now for not knowing five fives!

Dr Armitage was concerned about other needs too. He set up a Samaritan fund to help blind people who fell ill or on hard times. And more. He was largely responsible for setting up a college for the blind. He personally provided a swimming pool and gym equipment. And he arranged a special garden for the blind to be part of Kew Gardens.

And today the work he began has grown into a large organisation called the Royal National Institute for the Blind, or RNIB, which trains blind people to do all kinds of jobs, such as computer programming, or helps them set up their own businesses. It runs care homes and holidays for the blind, and much, much more.

And it all began – where? It began with a man who stopped thinking of the "can'ts" in his life and started thinking of the "cans".

TIME OF REFLECTION

We can all think of things that we'd really like to do but can't. Of course, some "can'ts" would become "cans" if we practised hard enough. But some things we'll never be able to do, so let's not think about them. Let's think about our "cans". What's your biggest "can" – the thing you do best? It could be in sport or in music or in school work or a hobby, or something like encouraging others like the boy in the first story. How in the next week or month are you going to make the most of it – for your own sake, and for others? Let's think about that for a moment.

BIBLE BITS

God has given us all the possibility of having a satisfying life, a life where the "can'ts" aren't so important.

David said in one of the Psalms:

"You have done many things for us, O Lord our God ... You have made many wonderful plans for us."

(Psalm 40:5)

And Jesus said:

"I have come in order that you might have life – life in all its fullness."

(John 10:10)

PRAYER

Help us, Lord, not to be jealous of those who can do what we can't. Thank you for what we *can* do. Help us to put our "cans" to good use, whether it's cheering on the sidelines like Robbie or helping in a way we hadn't thought of, like Thomas Armitage. Amen

VARIATION ON A THEME

Pupils – and teachers? – could share one thing they'd like to be able to do, but can't, and one thing they can (and perhaps show a result – a piece of work, a medal, etc). Include a good variety of "cans".

QUIZ QUESTIONS

1. Why was Thomas Armitage so depressed?
2. What pulled him out of this depression?
3. What was stopping blind people reading everything printed for them?
4. Who invented the reading system Dr Armitage chose?
5. What nationality was Louis Braille?
6. How old was he when he invented the system?
7. Braille uses patterns of – up to how many dots?
8. What does RNIB stand for?
9. Name one way the RNIB helps blind people.
10. Name one more.

The address of the RNIB is: 224 Great Portland Street, London W1N 6AA

NICKY CRUZ

God cares about us – gangs in New York

Other themes: peer pressure, self-esteem

THE PROBLEM

Here's something to think about. Listen to this.

Michelle sat gazing into her bedroom mirror. A miserable face gazed back. She spent a lot of her time like this, perhaps checking she was really there. For no one at school seemed to notice her, not as much as she wanted anyway. And she didn't have much in the way of friends.

"You," she said to her reflection, "could disappear one day and no one would notice."

She saw a tear squeezing out from under an eyelid so she turned to get a tissue. Her eyes fell on her pop magazine. The new girl group, Blaze, was on the cover. Her favourite was Kim, the one on the left with the big, dangly earrings. Bet she got noticed, thought Michelle.

And then the idea came. Could she do it? Course. She'd have to go the whole way. Hair cut really, really short, big earrings and, what else? She looked at the picture again. Long pink socks. They'd look odd with the school uniform, but that was the point.

The teacher would tell her to get back to normal, of course. But... yeah, she could be a bit cheeky, say, "No, why should I?" Yeah, that'd get her noticed. Not so cheeky that Mum would get called in, of course, just enough to build up a bit of a reputation.

Yeah, the new Michelle – Michelle the Cool, Michelle the Star.

Now think:

Will Michelle's plan get her more friends? Will it make her happy? Is there a better way?

(You could discuss this or pass on to the main story.)

THE STORY

Our true story today, about Nicky Cruz, is quite different from Michelle's, but deep down they have a similar problem. It opens in a school...

Nicky just couldn't stand it any more. If the teacher couldn't keep order, he'd do it. And he'd do it his way. This other boy in his class was a pain. So Nicky would teach him a lesson. Before anyone could stop him, he'd lifted a chair high in the air and brought it crashing down on the boy's head.

When the Headteacher threatened to phone the police, Nicky shouted back, "Do it and I'll kill you." Then he stormed out of the school.

It was the same wherever he went. He just seemed to boil over. Even when he was young, back home in Puerto Rico, he'd been trouble. His parents couldn't wait to see the back of him, so when he was fifteen he was pushed on a plane to New York to go and live with his brother Frank.

But just as school couldn't control him, nor could Frank. Nicky couldn't stand anyone telling him what to do. So he left.

Now he was on his own, angry with the world, but also lonely and frightened. He wandered the streets, no place to go, no friend to call on, no money to spend. He felt the icy wind come howling down between the rows of skyscrapers, felt it stir up the rotting litter in the streets and throw it at him to torment him. He saw figures slumped in alleys, drunk, asleep... or worse. He glimpsed faces looking down at him from lit windows, then turning away. They weren't interested in him.

He was shivering now, he needed a room badly. So – he mugged someone in the street for the rent money. Well, if he didn't help himself, who would? Who cared about Nicky? No one ever has, he thought, no one.

Then one day, while he was just mooching about, he saw them, a group of lads, dancing in the street to music, laughing. They were wearing black jackets with two blood-red Ms on the back. Nicky gazed at them until they shouted over, "This is Mau Mau territory. You don't belong here. Get lost, man."

No, no one wanted him.

Then he saw them again, at a party he'd drifted into. The Mau Mau gang. He pleaded to join. The leader told him, "You understand, if you join, it's for ever. If you try to leave, we'll kill you. But are you tough enough to be a Mau Mau? There's a test. Five of us will beat you up. If you survive, you're in."

Nicky survived, just. He came round from the beating with a broken nose, blood everywhere. But he was in. That's what mattered. He belonged.

Over the next weeks the Mau Maus, and there were over a hundred of them, were involved in murders, robberies and gangland fights. And Nicky was up there at the front, always ready to be more vicious, more reckless than his mates.

After six months he was elected leader of the gang. He'd made it – people noticed him now: now he was important. "I ain't afraid of nothing or no one," he boasted.

But deep down, he *was* still the same angry, lonely boy. And he was afraid. Afraid of the scary nightmares he kept getting, afraid of losing his tough reputation, afraid of what he was becoming. All the admiration, all the power, and he still wasn't happy.

Then he got an invitation to this Christian meeting. All the gangs did. Nicky refused to go, but someone asked, "Why? You afraid?" So he had to go.

To start with, the meeting was like a wild party. Members of different gangs were yelling at each other, some were disco dancing to the organ music, others were laughing or whistling. Then the preacher announced there'd be a collection and that the Mau Maus would come round for the money.

Yeah, thought Nicky, we'll collect it all right, then we'll run!

But when they'd collected the money, Nicky told his gang, "We're taking it to the preacher."

"What? You crazy, man?" But they knew not to argue, not with Nicky.

As Nicky sat down, he thought, Crazy? Yeah, I *was* crazy, but before, not now. For he'd just done something right and it felt good, better than all the bad things he'd done. For the preacher had trusted him, that hadn't happened before.

And in the hush that came over the hall, he listened to the preacher say, "God loves you. He wants to forgive you. He wants to change you." And Nicky realised that he did want to change. So that night, in front of his mates, Nicky walked to the front to become a Christian, to become the person God made him to be.

And he was changed. When later he was stabbed, he didn't want to take revenge. And he left the gang. It was dangerous but he did it.

Now he began to use his energy for good, saying to all the gangs he saw on the streets, to the drug addicts, to those at the bottom of the heap, "You can be changed. You're loved. You can be the person God made you to be."

He worked with a group which ran a centre where people could come and stay for a while, find someone to talk to, be helped off drugs – a place of safety and friendship. Nicky felt good belonging to a group which helped rather than hurt. Before, he'd just thought about himself – what do people think of *me*? And he was miserable. Now he was thinking of others. And he was happy.

And he no longer had to show off, to prove he was tough and cool and hard.

For he knew at last that someone cared about him. Now he could be himself.

TIME OF REFLECTION

Think for a second: Do you ever do things to get noticed? Show off a bit? Get a bit silly? You probably wouldn't do the things Nicky did, but do you ever pretend that you're tougher or smarter than you really are? It's good to remember that God loves us just as we are. We don't have to pretend to him. Just take a moment to think about this.

BIBLE BITS

Jesus tells us how valuable we are:

"Not one sparrow falls to the ground without your Father's consent ... So do not be afraid; you are worth much more than many sparrows."

(Matthew 10:29,31)

And God tells us that he, at least, doesn't worry too much about the image:

"Man looks at the outward appearance, but I look at the heart."
(I Samuel 16:7)

PRAYER

Thank you, Father, that we're all important to you, that we don't have to show off or do silly or bad things to get your attention. Amen

VARIATIONS ON A THEME

Pupils could create short sketches called, "Look at me, everyone!" about how showing off doesn't always have the desired effect. Take care that the atmosphere is right for THE STORY.

Alternatively, the story of David's anointing in 1 Samuel 16 could be acted out, showing how the tall, handsome ones got nowhere.

Run Baby Run, Nicky Cruz, is published by Hodder and Stoughton.

QUIZ QUESTIONS

1. How old was Nicky when he arrived in New York?
2. Why did he run away from school – and his brother?
3. How could you recognise a Mau Mau?
4. Why did Nicky want to join the gang?
5. Even as gang leader he was afraid – of what? (One thing)
6. Of what else?
7. Why did he go to the Christian meeting?
8. Why did he not run off with the collection money?
9. How did he prove he was a changed man? (One thing)
10. How else did he prove it?

JACKIE PULLINGER

Freedom from pressure to do wrong – teenagers in Hong Kong

Other themes: personal responsibility, drugs

THE PROBLEM

James has a real problem in this story. Listen and tell me what you'd advise him to do.

"So you know the rule," said the Dragon King. "Two Mars bars and you're in."

"And it's cold out here," said Tiger's Fang. "So hurry up."

James looked at the entrance to the supermarket. Just steal two Mars bars, and he'd be a member of the Dragon gang, for ever.

He'd been really surprised when they'd asked him to join the gang. He didn't have many friends as he was new to the school. So he'd said yes. Why not? He hadn't realised then they were into vandalising and nicking things. Anyway, he was glad he hadn't told his mum – she'd have made enquiries and found out they weren't the best of company. But they were company, and that's what he needed. People to go round with, do things with. He got lonely just being with Mum and his little brother.

To be accepted, he had to pass two tests. First he must drink Dragon's Blood, a revolting mixture of whisky, coke and tomato juice that the Dragon King, otherwise known as Nick Jones, had brought in a flask from home. And that was when the doubts began. He didn't want to drink it, it was stupid. But what choice did he have? If he backed out now, they'd make his life miserable at school, everyone would call him names. It would be unbearable. So he drank it. Now he stood outside the supermarket; it was the

43

final test. But he couldn't move. His feet seemed to be stuck to the pavement. And it wasn't only nerves. He just didn't want to do it.

"Go on then," said Tiger's Fang.

If only I'd said no to start with, thought James.

Now think:
What should James do? Is it really too late to say no? Or should he just go ahead and get it over with?

(You could discuss this or pass on to the main story.)

THE STORY

What if all your friends, everyone you knew, belonged to a particular gang? It would be even harder to say no then. What I'm going to tell you now is a true story.

Let me take you back about thirty years and to the other side of the world, to Hong Kong. We're going to a city within a city, for deep inside Hong Kong at that time was an area called the Walled City. Once it was a real walled city like a fort, with watchtowers and gateways. These have all gone. In fact you could walk up and down the busy streets which surround it and never find the way in. The Walled City doesn't welcome visitors.

The entrance is, in fact, a narrow slit between two tall buildings, and is guarded by a man sitting on a crate. If he lets you through, you will need to stop while your eyes adjust to the darkness. For the alley is like a tunnel, pierced only here and there by blades of light from the sky above. The sun is the least welcome visitor of all.

Now you can just make out the filthy, ramshackle buildings on either side. So move ahead. Careful! The alley is an open sewer. There are only two toilets for the thirty thousand people who live here, so most people... don't bother queuing. Just hope that no one decides to empty his bucket as you pass beneath his window. And don't step on the rotting food. Or the dead rats.

You can hear the clack and clatter of machines behind the closed doors – there are many one-room factories here where young children work long hours. But then you turn a corner, and there's an unearthly silence. Suddenly you see a face at a window. Someone is peering out at you. Dare you go further...?

So what kind of person lives in the Walled City? Some are ordinary people who have known no other home or life, but some are people on the run – refugees escaping from China, criminals escaping from the police, drug addicts trying to escape from their hard lives.

The Walled City is controlled by Triads, originally Chinese secret societies, now just criminal gangs. The two main gangs are the Ging Yu and the 14K. Children are recruited at an early age. The gang offers them a feeling of belonging and a feeling of safety. In return they must take part in all kinds of wrong activities, especially helping in the drug dens. They could well become drug addicts themselves.

In 1966 an English girl called Jackie Pullinger arrived in Hong Kong. She came because she believed that was where God wanted her. She got a job teaching music at a girls' college but felt drawn more and more to the Walled City. She remembered that Jesus had said to his followers, "You are the light of the world." The Chinese call the Walled City "Hak Nam" which means darkness. A good place then to be light.

She decided to open a youth club, to give the young people somewhere to go which was not run by gangsters and where there were no drugs on offer. It was just a bare room with benches and some games equipment, but they thought it was great. By now Jackie had given up the teaching job. She wanted to give herself full time to the people of the Walled City. She wanted to show them how much Jesus cared.

Let me tell you about two of the boys who came to the club.

Christopher lived with his family in one room above a chicken shed. They had two small bunk beds for eight people.

Christopher was about to join the 14K gang. It was expected. But part of him didn't want to join. He didn't want to be pushed into doing wrong things all his life. But what choice was there?

Jackie told him he did have a choice. Jesus was there to help people like him. Jesus could give him everything a gang could offer – and more. Christopher jumped at the chance. He became a Christian. He told the 14K leaders he didn't want to join the gang.

It was the first time they'd heard anything like that. And Jesus did give him more than the gang could – friends who would be good for him and who really cared.

Ah Ping, on the other hand, had joined the Triads at age 12. Now, at age 16, he was a hardened criminal. He'd done terrible things. But deep down he hated what he had become. When Jackie told him, even after all he'd done, Jesus still loved him and was ready to forgive him, he couldn't understand it, but he knew it was his only chance to change. He grabbed it.

Soon after this he was mugged and beaten up. But he decided not to take revenge – he knew being a Christian meant living a different way.

Several years ago the Walled City was pulled down, and the area is now a park. But Jackie's work goes on. She has set up houses all over Hong Kong where homeless people, some of whom are refugees, can be cared for, and where those who've come off drugs can be healed and grow up in enough aspects of thier life to relate back to society.

And now Jackie has been awarded the MBE for her work, for her willingness to let her light shine in a very dark place, for telling the people of the Walled City they do have a choice.

TIME OF REFLECTION

Think now: have you ever been tempted to do something wrong because it's expected or because people around would look down on you if you didn't go along with them? You don't have to say yes, you know. Like Christopher and Ah Ping, you do have a choice. But you need to be strong on the inside to say no. Are you able to do that? God can help you if you ask. Just a moment of silence while we think about this.

BIBLE BITS

Listen to what the Bible says:

"For God has said, 'I will never leave you; I will never abandon you.' Let us be bold, then, and say, 'The Lord is my helper, I will not be afraid. What can anyone do to me?'"

(Hebrews 13:5,6)

Jesus said, "Whoever follows me will have the light of life and will never walk in darkness."

(John 8:12)

PRAYER

Lord Jesus, thank you that Jackie was there when Christopher and Ah Ping needed help, and thank you that *you* were there to make them strong on the inside. Sometimes we too can get into difficult situations where it's hard to say no, but thank you that, if we ask, you can make us strong like them, to spread light rather than darkness. Amen.

VARIATIONS ON A THEME

The early part of the main story – the walk through the Walled City – could be mimed by a group of children. Jackie Pullinger's book, *Chasing the Dragon* (Hodder and Stoughton, 1980), gives more information about the area. The description here is based on my own visit.

Or groups of children could perform their own plays on the same theme as THE PROBLEM, perhaps stopping at the point of decision – to go with the crowd or to say no.

QUIZ QUESTIONS

1. The Walled City was part of which large city?
2. What was Jackie's first job in Hong Kong?
3. Hak Nam means – ?
4. Jesus said, "You are the – "?
5. Christopher lived above a – ?
6. When he refused to join the 14K gang, why were the leaders so surprised?
7. How old was Ah Ping when he joined the Triads?
8. How old was he when he became a Christian?
9. Why did Ah Ping not want to take revenge after he was mugged?
10. Which honour was Jackie awarded?

ELIZABETH FRY

Freedom from fears – caring for the prisoners in Newgate

Other themes: courage, faith

THE PROBLEM

Listen to this and see what you think.

Katy was having second thoughts. She hadn't realised how it would look from up here. It was a long, long way down. Why on earth had she signed up for this? Oh, she knew why really – she'd wanted to try abseiling for ages, her friends had all done it and thought it was great.

But suddenly it seemed stupid, pointless. Why couldn't she use the stairs? Why go down the *wall*?

Steve, the instructor, could see the hesitation, no – more than hesitation: this was fear. "You don't have to do it, you know," he said quietly. "I assure you you're perfectly safe. But it's up to you."

Katy longed to say, "Yes, I'll do it." And she knew she'd regret it if she turned away now.

But – it was a long, long way down.

Now think:
What should she do? What would you do? Have you ever been in a situation like this, where your fear could stop you doing something you really want to?

(You could discuss this or pass on to the main story.)

THE STORY

Our true story begins about two hundred years ago, in London. A fashionable city, but also a dangerous one. A city of wide thoroughfares, but also of dark alleys, *very* dark alleys. There were areas where no one wandered alone, areas where anything could happen – and usually did.

But only one spot in London was known as "Hell above ground". It was the worst place of all. Our story is about a woman who went there. Alone.

Sshh... listen... there's her carriage now...

The horse-drawn carriage shudders its way over the rough ground. Perhaps the woman inside is shuddering too. But that would be from the deathly cold, not from fear. Oh yes, part of her is afraid – for she knows she may be attacked, even killed. But deep down she has peace. For she has, with God's help, faced her fears many times before this and God has never let her down. And she knows God has sent her to this place, this "Hell above ground". He will protect her.

Through the window she sees a road-sweeping boy scuttling out of the way of the horse. Then she sees – it. Her destination. Newgate Prison, looking like a hideous black castle. Only a few streets from St Paul's Cathedral, but another world, a darker world.

The carriage stops and she gets down. Pulling her grey shawl more tightly around her, she mounts the steps to a heavy shoulder-height door topped with iron spikes, through which a shadowy figure peers at her.

She is recognised. The door swings open, slams shut behind her. She is inside. Inside the dreaded Newgate Prison. This is the lodge, the way in, and for the very fortunate, the way out. But she must go further than this. She gazes at the handcuffs and cruel leg irons hanging on the wall while the guard unbolts a massive inner door. Another guard slides from the shadows and without a word leads her down a long dark passage. She has been in Newgate several times before, but never to "Hell above ground".

Anyone who'd known her as a child would be surprised to see her here, for she had been the timid one, the one who was so afraid of the dark, who jumped at loud noises. She had ten brothers and sisters, all bright and boisterous; only Betsy, as she was called then, was full of fears.

But as she grew up she realised there was someone who could help her overcome her fears. God. She was glad, for she didn't want to spend all her life being afraid. Her family were Quakers, Christians who had their own kind of church, called a Meeting House. But Betsy wanted to take it more seriously than her family seemed to.

So she married a strict Quaker, Joseph Fry, and moved to London. But life was unexpectedly dull. She wanted to *do* something for God. But what? Back home in Norfolk she'd done things – visiting sick people and cooking for them, starting a little school for the poor local children. Bedraggled and often smelly they were, but she loved them – "Betsy's Imps" they were known as – and they loved her and the wonderful Bible stories she read to them. Surely in a big city there was something like that she could do.

Then a visitor came to the Fry home and told her about Newgate Prison, how the conditions were so terrible, how, because their mothers were prisoners, there were children there, babies even, unfed, unclothed. Betsy, or Elizabeth as she was called now, got together a group of Quaker friends and began knitting baby clothes. At last – something to do!

On that first visit she went to the Women's Infirmary, the prison hospital. She was horrified. There were no beds. A few of the women and children had some dirty straw, but most were lying on the cold, bare boards. She saw no sign of medicines, no place to wash properly.

She was overwhelmed by their need – and, when she gave them the clothes, overwhelmed by their gratitude too. Somebody cared – they'd forgotten that. Yes, Elizabeth told them, God cares, and I care too. She knew they were prisoners, but knew too the innocent were mixed in with the guilty, knew that people were arrested for anything. Why, you could be hanged for stealing a loaf of bread, or a shirt from a washing line.

She visited the infirmary again and again. And she learnt that elsewhere in the prison were hundreds of other women, living in even worse conditions, living in a place called by the jailers, "Hell above ground".

And now, she is here. The jailers in this section are astonished to see her, to hear her request. To go in there – alone? Into "Hell above ground"?

"Oh, madam, you don't understand."

"I understand," she says. "Now please open the door."

She can hear them already: mad laughter that threatens never to stop, shrieks of agony, a hundred other voices, shouting, arguing, singing.

The jailers open the door. And she walks in. The sight is incredible. Two women are fighting on the floor, tearing at each other's hair. A child is slumped in a corner, dressed only in filth. A young woman, clearly starving, rocks a baby, trying to stop its sobs. The mad laughter is still going on. But then everyone seems mad, mad with despair.

Then they notice her and there is total silence. Even the laughing stops.

And Elizabeth knows this is the moment of most danger. They could so easily rush at her, tear at her clothes, her hair, in jealousy or in rage.

But they don't. They see something in her eyes, something they barely recognise. Can it be love?

She moves over to the filthy child and smiles.

And the child smiles back.

Before long she has gathered the women together, told them that she wants to do something for them, for their children. To start a school. Right there in the prison. Yes, yes, they say.

So Elizabeth returns with books and helpers, and the school – for thirty children – begins. The mothers crowd round, wanting to learn too. So more helpers are brought in, the women taught not just to read, but also to sew, so that if and when they are released they will have an honest way of getting money.

The schooldays begin and end with Elizabeth reading Bible stories. The prisoners love them as much as the Imps did.

The prison authorities, even Parliament, are astonished at the change in "Hell above ground". In fact Elizabeth Fry became so well known that tourists would arrive at the prison asking to see her reading the Bible.

It was just the beginning. She helped improve conditions in other prisons, not just in England, but in France and Germany and other countries too, and on the convict ships that took thousands of women prisoners to Australia. Wherever she saw a need, she did something. She set up libraries for the bored men in coastguard stations. She founded the first professional group of nurses – the "Fry nurses" as they were known. And lots more.

All because she would not allow her fears to take over her life. When she felt afraid of doing something, if it was a good and right thing to do, then she prayed for courage and got on and did it – and felt less afraid the next time.

For God was with her. And didn't he do wonderful things through her?

TIME OF REFLECTION

Some fears are good to have – God does not want us taking silly risks or playing dangerous games. But some fears can stop us enjoying life to the full or stop us doing something for other people. What are you afraid of? God can help us if we ask. He wants us to enjoy life, not be afraid of it.

Just take a moment to think about this.

BIBLE BITS

David, often in lonely dark places looking after his sheep, could say,

"Even if I go through the deepest darkness,
I will not be afraid, Lord,
for you are with me."

(Psalm 23:4)

And God himself said,

"Do not be afraid! I am with you...
I will make you strong and help you."

(Isaiah 41:10)

PRAYER

In the Bible, Father, many of the heroes were afraid at times – Moses, Gideon, even your son, Jesus. Yet you stood by them and helped them face their fears and overcome them. Help us when we're afraid, to know that you're there, ready to give us courage and strength. Amen

VARIATIONS ON A THEME

Perhaps there is an adult known to the children who can talk about a time when they were afraid and God helped.

Or you could tell the story of Moses' call at the burning bush, how God understood his anxiety and boosted his confidence.

QUIZ QUESTIONS

1. How many brothers and sisters did Elizabeth Fry have?
2. How was she different?
3. She started a little school in Norfolk – what were her pupils known as?
4. Why was she unhappy at first in London?
5. What did she do when she heard about Newgate?
6. What was bad about the Women's Infirmary?
7. Why were the jailers to the women's prison unwilling to open the door?
8. Why was she not more afraid?
9. Why did tourists want to visit Newgate?
10. She improved conditions on the convict ships bound for – where?

TERRY WAITE

Freedom can have too great a cost – held hostage in Beirut

Other themes: is violence ever right? revenge, bullying, loneliness

THE PROBLEM

Listen to this. What would you do in this situation?

Three-thirty at last. Jamie unlocked his bike to cycle home. Glancing up he could see big Sam Baynes coming across the school playground – he looked in a foul mood, and Jamie could guess why: he'd seen Sam standing outside the Head's office. Good, thought Jamie grinning, Sam's a bully, deserved any punishment he got.

The next thing he knew was a fist slamming into his stomach. "That'll wipe the smile off," Sam called back as he strode off.

Walking his bike through the school gates, Jamie couldn't stop the tears coming.

"What's up, Jamie?" It was his older brother, Rob, cycling past from the high school up the road. Usually Rob ignored him, but he could see Jamie was in a state.

Jamie explained, pointing to Sam's disappearing figure.

"Well," said Rob. "Let's get him now. Tell you what, I'll hold him while you give him a punch like he gave you. Then I'll smack him around a bit. He won't give you any trouble after that."

Jamie thought. He wasn't sure it would work out like that – and wouldn't it make him just as much of a bully as Sam?

Now think:
What should Jamie do? If he and his brother set on Sam, would that definitely solve the problem as Rob thinks it will,

or could it make things worse? Think too if the use of fists is the best way, the right way, of dealing with the problem.

(You could discuss this or pass on to the main story.)

THE STORY

Keep that in mind as I tell you now a true story about someone who had the opportunity to use violence to solve his problem.

They said they would lead him to the place where the hostages were being held.

They said, "Come with us, come and meet the kidnappers, we will help you work out a deal." It seemed like they could be trusted.

Terry didn't realise he was walking into a trap.

Terry Waite had a special role in the Church of England as the envoy, or agent, of the Archbishop of Canterbury. When people abroad were in danger or difficulty, he could be sent out to help. Now he was in the war-torn Middle East, in Beirut, where one of the fighting groups had kidnapped several British people. Their idea was to bribe Britain into helping them against their enemies. Terry's task was to make contact with the kidnappers and persuade them to release the hostages, then get them to safety.

Terry would have made quite an impression when he landed in Beirut in that January of 1987 – six foot seven, almost seventeen stone, wearing size fourteen shoes. But he knew he would have to tread very carefully not to put the hostages in even more danger.

So far, so good. He had talked with people who knew who the kidnappers were and where the hostages were being held. "Trust us, we'll take you to them," these people said. Now Terry was sitting, blindfolded, in the back seat of a car, being driven through the dark streets of Beirut.

Unaware that the trap was closing.

The car stopped in a small road full of potholes. He was led to an upstairs room and told to wait. "When will I see the hostages?" he asked. They just said, "Later."

Still blindfolded, he waited, hoping against hope. Finally he slept.
"Stand up, Mr Waite." It was the evening of the second day.

Terry felt himself being guided back down the stairs and into a van. "Are you taking me to the hostages?"

They answered, "Don't speak."

When the van stopped he was led into a garage. The blindfold was off now and he could see an open trapdoor in the floor. He was taken through it to a large underground room. In one wall was a heavy steel door with a barred window. The door swung open to reveal an empty cell. He was pushed in. He heard the key turned in the lock behind him. And knew that he had been betrayed. They were not going to take him to see the hostages, they were not going to help him work out a deal. No. Terry was now a hostage himself.

The days dragged by, the cell stiflingly hot, the air smelling of petrol and sweat. The kidnappers brought him food but didn't answer his questions – why? how long? Terry spent much time in prayer, for his family, for the other hostages, and for himself: God, help me, please, help me.

Then one day he was blindfolded and led out. For a moment he thought excitedly, Am I to be set free? But no, he was simply taken to another cell where he was kept chained, released just once a day to be taken to the toilet. One time he was tortured, beaten across the soles of his feet till they burnt like fire. His captors seemed to think he had some vital information. But he didn't.

The days passed. He went on praying. How long? ... Why? ... God, help me!

Then, one day, when he was taken to the bathroom, pushed in with the usual "Be quick!", he saw, on top of the toilet cistern, a gun. An automatic pistol, complete with silencer. His mind was racing. Obviously one of the guards had just been to the toilet and left his gun behind. Perhaps tired or just careless. Whatever, Terry realised that there, within reach, was his way out. His guard was standing unsuspecting outside the door. Oh, perhaps there were one or two other guards around as well, but he had surprise on his side. He could do it. He could escape. It was his chance, his only chance.

But he knew, if he picked up the gun, he would have to be prepared to use it. He wouldn't get away just waving it around. He would have to hurt someone, even kill them. And he knew he couldn't do it. He had always believed that violence was wrong. It would be wrong now. Even though *they* had hurt *him*.

He called the guard in, pointed out the gun. The guard grabbed at it, took it out of Terry's reach. Terry had given away his only chance of escape.

He was to stay in captivity for a long time after that, most of it chained up and alone. He suffered constant toothache, cockroaches biting his feet as he tried to sleep, and terrible loneliness. But he never regretted not using the gun.

He was released in November 1991 after 1,763 days in captivity.

That's nearly five years.

But he never regretted not using the gun.

TIME OF REFLECTION

Think now: is it ever right to use violence? Don't just think of the violence of fists and weapons but the violence of cruel words. Is it ever right to hurt? Does violence solve problems or can it just make things worse? What would you have done in Terry's place? What could have been the result for him, for the other hostages?

Just a moment of silence while we think about these things.

BIBLE BITS

Listen to what the Bible says:

"If someone has done you wrong, do not repay him with a wrong."

(Romans 12:17)

Jesus said: "Love your enemies and pray for those who persecute you."

(Matthew 5:44)

PRAYER

Father God, next time I have the opportunity to hurt someone, help me to think whether it's the right thing to do, whatever they've done to me. Thank you for Jesus, who never hit back, who never said a cruel word, who even prayed for his executioners, "Father, forgive them." Amen

VARIATION ON A THEME

The story about Terry Waite could be mimed by a group of children as you read. You would need a minimum of three actors (Waite, contact, guard) plus a blindfold.

QUIZ QUESTIONS

1. Who was Terry Waite working for when he went to the Middle East?
2. What had he been sent to do?
3. What size shoes does he take?
4. When did he know for sure that he had been led into a trap?
5. What did Terry spend much time doing?
6. Where did he see the gun?
7. Why did he not use it to escape?
8. What was the pain inside his head due to?
9. What made it difficult to sleep?
10. For how long was he held hostage?

CS LEWIS

(but don't tell children the name yet)

Freedom of the imagination – writing the Narnia books

Other themes: the value of fiction, using our creative talents

THE PROBLEM

A teacher has a bit of a problem in this story. Listen and think who's right: teacher or pupil.

"Robert, could you come and see me, please?"

Robert looked up from the Science book he was reading. Uh, oh – Mr Turner was frowning. He got up and walked to the teacher's desk. Some of his classmates were looking up now. It was always fun to hear someone else get told off.

"Robert, what is this? I asked you to write a story about a journey to an unknown planet and what you've given me is simply a list of facts about Mars."

Robert pushed his glasses further up his nose and announced, "I've given up writing stories. They're silly."

"Oh. I see," said Mr Turner, sighing. "And why, tell me, are they silly exactly?"

Up went the glasses again. "They're not true, you see. Stories are made up. They're pointless. You can't learn anything from stuff which isn't true. So I'm just going to read and write facts from now on."

"Well, Robert," murmured Mr Turner, "we'll just have to see about that, won't we?"

Now think:

Is Robert right? Are stories silly and pointless because they're not true? What is the point of reading and writing stories?

(You could discuss this or pass on to the main – true! – story.)

THE STORY

Stories, in fact, are enjoyed all over the world. In North Africa, as darkness falls, a storyteller will settle himself in the town square, light his lamp and place it on the ground. Young and old will gather round and whole worlds will come to life in the flickering light. In Indonesia, storytellers will use shadow puppets to share tales of battles and bloodshed and incredible heroism.

Storytelling is nothing new. Go back two thousand years and we find a man travelling round, telling stories of a house built on sand, a friend who comes at midnight, a lost sheep. Yes – I'm talking about Jesus, who called his stories "parables" – stories with a meaning. They're very special stories.

In this country stories are usually written down. Perhaps you've turned over the pages wondering what will happen next to the Famous Five or Harry Potter or Matilda... or the children in Narnia.

Jack loved stories. Jack wasn't his real name, but when he was four, he suddenly announced, "I want to be called Jacksie" – or Jack for short. Perhaps you can guess his real name before we come to it.

Jack was born in 1898 and spent his childhood in Northern Ireland. He loved the adventure of cycling with his older brother Warren over the hills around Belfast. But even more of an adventure was exploring the family house – a world of spiders' webs and creaking floorboards, where a hidden door could, with just a little imagination, lead to a secret passage, or where a dusty sea-chest could contain great treasure.

In fact Jack had more than "a little imagination". After he'd heard a story about there being a pot of gold at the end of the rainbow, he got the idea that rainbows ended in the middle of the front garden path. So – he started digging. He dug and dug and dug. But – no gold. So he went indoors, leaving a deep hole. It was dark when Dad came home from work... He opened the garden gate, strode towards the front door, and... you can imagine the rest.

Jack especially loved two kinds of story: adventures with brave knights or explorers, and fantasy stories in which animals spoke and acted like people. A favourite was Beatrix Potter's *Squirrel Nutkin*.

The stories he wrote himself rolled the two kinds into one. They were filled with characters like Sir Peter Mouse and King Bunny of Animal-land.

Eventually he was sent to boarding school. He hated it: the Headmaster was a bully, the lessons incredibly boring. But he could escape into books. He had gone on to science fiction by now, especially anything with travel to other worlds.

Later he went on to University in Oxford where he was much happier. He was such a good scholar that he became a lecturer there.

It was a busy, satisfying life, but what Jack really looked forward to were Thursday evenings, when the Inklings met. The Inklings were what Jack and his friends called themselves when they got together to discuss, yes, that's right, books. They would often read their own stories, hopefully to the approval and applause of the rest of the group.

Another Inkling was JRR Tolkien who wrote *The Hobbit* and *Lord of the Rings*. It was Professor Tolkien who encouraged Jack's interest in another book, the Bible. Jack had been forced to go to church when he was small, but nothing about the services was designed to appeal to a young boy and he was bored. It had really put him off Christianity. But now he began to see what an adventure being a Christian could be.

And after a lot of thought, he became one, on the way to the zoo, in fact – but that's another story!

Jack was writing a lot now: a science fiction novel, books for students, and books explaining what he believed and why.

Then came World War Two. Jack enjoyed having evacuees staying in his house – children who'd been sent, or evacuated, to the countryside where they'd be safe from the bombing. It was an old rambling house so they didn't get in the way. But he was sad that the children became bored so easily. They just didn't seem to like books, didn't seem to have much imagination.

Then one day one of the children found an old wardrobe. "What's behind it?" she asked. "Can I look inside?"

And Jack thought about that wardrobe and had an idea – an idea for a story which *would* interest children, that would stop them being bored, that would help them love books. Then perhaps he thought, "Do I have time? Shouldn't I be working on more serious stuff?"

He decided, no, he did have time, for stories were important – they could fill a mind with wonder, and get across important things, like how to be brave and generous, and they could help children understand spiritual things too – sacrifice and heaven and eternal life.

So he began. "Let's see..." he thought, "I want some talking animals, of course – mm, a faun... with a red scarf and an umbrella – yes, and a beaver who's afraid of something, and a lion who's afraid of nothing and who will be ready to give his life for others. And I know how to begin all right – with the wardrobe!"

Can you guess what this story became? Yes, *The Lion, the Witch and the Wardrobe.* And the boy who demanded to be called Jack was its author, CS Lewis.

(This would be a good point to read a little of the book itself, perhaps the first paragraph, and then Lucy going through the wardrobe a couple of pages later.)

The book wasn't finished for a long time, but it was quickly followed by other Narnia stories: *Prince Caspian, The Voyage of the 'Dawn Treader'* – which took only two months to write – then *The Silver Chair, The Horse and his Boy, The Magician's Nephew* and finally *The Last Battle.* Together they're known as *The Chronicles of Narnia.*

Millions have loved and read these books. They were written for children, who want to know what lies beyond the darkness at the back of the wardrobe, and aren't afraid to find out.

TIME OF REFLECTION

Let's think about the stories we've enjoyed most and the stories we've enjoyed writing ourselves. Isn't it good that God gave us imaginations? But perhaps you use your imagination best in other ways, like in painting or acting or in dance or movement. In any case let's think for a moment about the best we've done and the best others have done.

BIBLE BITS

The Bible reminds us that not all stories are good for us. We have to be careful, perhaps especially when choosing stories on video. The Bible says:

"Fill your minds with those things that are good and that deserve praise: things that are ... right, pure ... and honourable."
(Philippians 4:8)

PRAYER

Thank you for the stories we enjoy reading or hearing, and thank you that you've given us our imagination to make stories of our own. Thank you too for the stories Jesus told all those years ago that can still mean so much to people today. Amen.

VARIATION ON A THEME

Acting out several of Jesus' parables would be an appropriate addition – either scripted or vigorously mimed while the Bible verses are read.

QUIZ QUESTIONS

1. Name Jack's brother.
2. Why did Jack dig up the garden path?
3. Jack wrote about a Sir Peter – what animal was he?
4. What did the Inklings do?
5. Why did Jack not feel good about Christianity when he was young?
6. But he became a Christian – on the way to the – what?
7. What gave him the idea for a story in which children go through a wardrobe?
8. The faun has a red scarf and – what?
9. Why did he want talking animals in his story?
10. Which of the books took only two months to write?

MARY SLESSOR

Bullying isn't right! – tribal practices in Africa

Other themes: courage, not turning away when someone needs you

THE PROBLEM

Listen to this. What would you do in this situation?

Joe wandered into the dining hall and looked round. With his best friend away he'd have to find some other company. He'd feel a right nerd sitting by himself.

Well... there was bully boy Derek Harris and his stupid gang. They'd have to do. He strolled over, sat down and opened his lunch box.

Derek was going on about a little lad in the class called Mark Fenton. "But what really did it was when Fenton told Mr Jones that I'd stuck chewing gum behind the bookcase. What stinking business was it of his? Tell you what..." – his gang gathered in closer – "he needs to learn a lesson, he does. And I'm gonna be his teacher."

The gang were impressed. "Whatcha gonna do, Delboy?"

"I'll tell you. He has to go down this little alley on the way home. I'll be there with a great slodge of well-chewed gum. He'll be scraping it off for weeks!"

The gang chuckled and went, "Yeah, yeah." Then there were the sounds of crisp packets being scrunched up and chairs pushed back.

Joe looked up and found Derek looming over him. Derek spoke softly. "I guess you heard all that, but you just keep quiet about it. It's not your business, all right?"

Joe shrugged his shoulders. Well, it wasn't his business. Or was it?

Now think:
What should Joe do? Is it right that he "keeps quiet" about it, if he just lets it happen? Or does he have a responsibility towards Mark Fenton?

(You could discuss this or pass on to the main story.)

THE STORY

Keep Joe's problem in mind as I tell you a true story, about Mary Slessor from Scotland.

Mary could hear them following her in the darkness, hear the rapid clickety-clack of their clogs on the cobbles as they gained on her. She'd been warned that part of Dundee could be dangerous but, young as she was, she'd been determined to help out at the Christian youth club held there.

They were right behind her now.

Suddenly she was surrounded. A gang of rough lads. The leader began spinning a lead weight on a piece of string round his head, letting the string out little by little. "We don't want your sort here," he breathed. "So get out – now!"

She stared at him. She could see the lead getting closer, closer to her face at each spin. Swish... swish... She could feel the quick sigh of air as it whisked by her forehead. But if she ran off now, how would the young people living in these dark streets ever hear of a God who loved and valued them? So, her heart pounding, her lips whispering a prayer, she stood her ground.

The lad finally let the weight fall to his side and laughed. "You're a brave one!"

"But what about you?" she answered back. "Are you brave? Brave enough to come to the club?"

They came.

She'd won.

As Mary grew up she longed to go as a missionary to Africa. And in 1876, when she was 27, she boarded the ship *Ethiopia* for the long voyage. She knew Calabar, on Africa's west coast, was full of diseases and dangers, but God had told her to go, and that, for Mary, was that.

She loved Calabar, loved climbing its trees to feel the breeze whooshing through the topmost branches, loved its sunsets, great streaks of flame across the sky, loved its children who became her friends.

She could have done without some of the animal population though. She had only just landed when an iguana, a kind of huge lizard, seven feet long, scurried up to her, hissing horribly. She raised her umbrella, ready to do battle, and it scuttled off.

Another time an elephant charged at her. She prayed... and it changed course just in time.

And one night she woke up to find a long python slithering across her bedroom floor. A smack on the nose made it realise Mary was no easy victim. It went!

But more horrifying than any creature were the tribal customs – like human sacrifices to please the gods. But the custom that saddened Mary most was the killing of baby twins. It was believed the presence of twins brought bad luck, so as soon as they were born they were taken out into the jungle and left to die.

Mary prayed: Lord, I can't just stand by and let this happen. But what can I do?

And God showed her.

She developed a network of spies who would rush to tell her if a woman was about to give birth. She would grab towels and medicines – and her umbrella, just in case – and run. If twins were born, she would bring them home with her straightaway to look after. She hung hammocks from the ceiling of her hut so she could rock them to sleep. And the people gradually learnt that twins do not bring bad luck.

But one of her most frightening times had nothing to do with wild animals or babies.

Mary heard that a woman from one of the villages was going to be punished. "What has she done?" Mary asked.

"She handed food to a man who was not her husband," she was told.

"How is that a crime? And what is her punishment?"

"She will have boiling oil poured on her."

That evening in the village it was like a great party. Flames danced from fires lit round the main square. You could hear drums over the laughter and shouting. Mary pushed her way through the crowd and saw what was in the middle of the square. A woman was lying on the ground, her hands and feet held by four men. Beside her was a steaming pot of palm oil. The witch doctor, his face painted bright yellow, filled a ladle with the oil and held it over the trembling woman.

And Mary had a second to think: Am I just going to stand by and watch this happen? She knew what God wanted her to do.

She rushed up to the witch doctor. "You can stop that now!" she announced.

The witch doctor stumbled back in surprise, the hot oil spilling onto his feet. As he hopped about yelping, Mary began pushing the four men away. "Let her go – now. Get away with you!" They realised this was someone you don't argue with and backed off. Mary bent down to help the shaking woman to her feet, then straightened up to see... wild eyes glaring from a mask of yellow.

The witch doctor! – holding high above his head the heavy ladle. Mary knew it could crack her skull like an egg.

He brought it down with a roar. It sliced the air to one side of Mary. Then the other side. Then he whirled it round his head, hoping to terrify her, hoping she would run, screaming, back into the jungle. But Mary remembered a boy with a lead weight many years before, and how she had stood her ground and won. God had protected her then. He would do the same now.

The witch doctor's lunges became wilder, his roaring louder. But Mary could see not just anger in his eyes, but fear too. Fear at a woman who did not fear him.

Finally, exhausted, he dropped the ladle and Mary led the woman to safety. After a day or two her "crime" had been forgotten and she returned home.

No one can count the number of lives Mary saved, or the number of babies she rescued, or the number of people she helped understand that God loved and valued them.

So much changed in that part of Africa.

All because of a woman who did not turn away when someone needed her.

TIME OF REFLECTION

Think now: have I let something bad or wrong happen when I could have done something about it? – someone being hurt when I could have at least told an adult about it, or someone feeling afraid or unhappy when I could have helped them or comforted them? Have I ever thought, "I can't be bothered?" Have I ever turned away when my help was needed?

Just a moment of silence while we think about these things.

BIBLE BITS

Listen to what the Bible says:

"Our love should not be just words and talk; it must be true love, which shows itself in action."

(I John 3:18)

"We must help the weak."

(Acts 20:35)

(Children could also be reminded of the Good Samaritan story – Luke 10.)

PRAYER

Father, when I see something happening that shouldn't be happening, help me not to turn away but to think – can I, should I, do something about it? We think of Mary's courage and pray for that courage for ourselves. Amen

VARIATION ON A THEME

THE PROBLEM – the dining hall scene – could be made into a play by a group of pupils – with a "freeze" as the "Now think" questions are read out.

QUIZ QUESTIONS

1. Why did Mary not run away when the gang in Dundee told her to?
2. What good thing happened because she didn't run away?
3. Why did she love Calabar's trees?
4. How big was the iguana?
5. How did Mary deal with the snake?
6. Why would a mother fear having twins?
7. What "crime" had the village woman committed?
8. How did the witch doctor try to frighten Mary?
9. How come Mary had the courage not to run away?
10. What happened to the village woman?

Note: Calabar is part of present day Nigeria.

SOJOURNER TRUTH / MARTIN LUTHER KING

Inequality isn't right! – racism in the U.S.

Other themes: slavery, bullying

THE PROBLEM

Listen to this and see what you think.

Simon leaned across the table and, making sure the teacher couldn't hear, said, "Hey, Mani, or whatever your name is, is it true that where you come from your tribe's only got one brain between them and you have to share it round? Eh?"

Mani, who'd only been in the class a few days, ignored the insult and got on with his work in silence. But then the teacher called him up to read.

"Oh, Mani, or whatever your name is," – Simon said that every time – "get him to teach you to speak proper English, will ya?" He turned and nudged Amjid sitting next to him.

Amjid knew what Mani was going through. It had only stopped for Amjid when the bullies learnt they weren't getting anywhere. Then they'd given up – and eventually he'd been accepted. But it had been rough.

Now Amjid had a choice. He longed to tell Simon to stop getting at Mani, but it was so much easier to go along with it. If he got on the wrong side of Simon and the gang, perhaps they'd start on him again.

Now think:
What should Amjid do? The easy thing, or the hard thing?

(You could discuss this or pass on to the main story.)

THE STORY

James and Betsey gazed down at their new baby. "Isabella," murmured Betsey, "my Isabella."

"Not your Isabella," whispered James fiercely. "The master's Isabella. She belongs to him. Nothing belongs to slaves like us."

Betsey sighed. She knew he was right. They were black slaves on a farm near New York in 1800 and that meant they were not even regarded as people, just property, to be bought and sold. She remembered how two of her children had been taken from her years before, literally carried from the slave house and driven away. The master had sold them, and she knew she would probably never see them again.

Betsey began to cry at the memory of it. For she was not "property" – she was a person, and people have feelings. And when your children are taken from you, it hurts, it really hurts.

However, the master liked Isabella, or Belle as she was known, for she grew up tall and strong, and able to work hard, and that was what mattered to him. For the moment she was safe.

But when she was about your age, the master died and the new owner decided to sell at auction some of the property – including Belle. She was sold to a shopkeeper who beat her, then to an innkeeper, then to a farmer. And all the time her hatred of white people grew and grew – she used to pray that God would kill them all.

Eventually she married, another slave of course, and had five children.

Then a law was passed: older slaves were to be freed. Free? Belle could hardly believe it. It was too good to be true, surely.

And it was. Her master refused to free her at the promised time. She was so angry she ran away, even though it meant leaving her family. Some friendly people took her in.

It was there that Belle met with God. She suddenly became aware of him all around her, and ashamed of the bad feelings which had built up in her heart. And she understood what Jesus had come to do, to clean away all this anger and hatred. She let him come into her life. It changed her for ever. The bitterness against white people just slipped away.

She started to go to church and was astonished how she was treated – as a person. Later on she managed to visit her children – her husband had died – but there was nothing she could do for them.

So she moved to New York and began work as a maid. But she wasn't satisfied. I may not be able to read or write, she thought, but isn't there something I can do for God, perhaps something to help those still in slavery?

And God told her what she could do. She could become a travelling preacher, go and tell the world how slavery was wrong, that it wasn't what God wanted. What? she must have thought – a black woman telling white people to change their way of life?

She made her decision. She chose not the easy thing but the hard thing. She would go. But she would take a new name – Sojourner Truth. A sojourner is someone who does not stay in one place for long, so that fitted, and Truth because Jesus said, "I am the truth", and she'd be speaking for him.

Other people, both black and white, were trying to put an end to slavery too. Some told slaves: "Rise up against your masters!" Sojourner would have nothing to do with this. Violence was not Jesus' way. She went instead to white people to reason with them, to try and change their attitudes.

Her message to a world that looked down on black people, especially black women, was: "Aren't I equal to any one of you in God's eyes? So why do you go against God?"

She was a born teacher. When she spoke, in meeting halls or in the open air, people listened all right. She was very tall, taller than most men, and had a quick, lively mind and a great sense of humour. And how she knew the Bible!

Of course, many jeered at her, some even threatened her life, but she understood – they'd been brought up to look down on black people, so she could forgive them.

She continued travelling and speaking until she was in her eighties. She had seen many changes in that time. For example, President Abraham Lincoln had taken up the cause of black people and passed a law to ban slavery. This was wonderful but in some states slave owners defied the law. Freed slaves were taken captive and dragged to states where slavery was still practised, and their children were carried off to become unpaid factory workers.

So Sojourner went on fighting. She longed for her country to honour God and treat all people fairly. Black people, she argued, have worked hard to make America rich, they should have rights the same as anyone.

Sojourner died in 1883. Both black and white were proud to have known her, glad she had brought them closer together.

Slavery was eventually stopped altogether, but the battle for equal rights had a long way to go. In each generation there were those who pleaded for justice for all, perhaps the most famous being Martin Luther King. He was a black Baptist minister in Alabama, one of the southern states. He felt that God wanted him to do something for his fellow blacks, who were not allowed, for example, to sit on certain seats in buses or in restaurants, their children not allowed to go to certain schools. So in the 1950s and '60s he organised peaceful protests.

For his trouble, his house was dynamited and he was arrested and sent to prison seventeen times. But he kept on, pleading with white people for justice, pleading with black people not to let their anger boil over. In Washington in 1963, 200,000 people, black and white, came together to march through the city for equal rights, and to hear Martin speak. It was a great occasion.

He just longed for all human beings to be treated equally. But some people hated him just as they'd hated Sojourner Truth. And five years after he spoke to that crowd, Martin Luther King was murdered.

But he had accomplished so much. Like Sojourner, he had brought people of different races closer together, taught them to see they had an equal place in the heart of God.

TIME OF REFLECTION

Have you ever looked down on someone because they were different from you in some way? Perhaps in the way they looked or the way they spoke, or perhaps because they were younger than you, or because they were very old, or because they had less money? Jesus never looked down on anyone, whatever their race, or appearance, or age – he treated them equally. Do you?

Just take a moment to think about that.

BIBLE BITS

In the Bible it says:

"For God loved *the world* so much that he gave his only Son, so that *everyone* who believes in him may not die but have eternal life."

(John 3:16)

"... be peaceful and friendly, and always... show a gentle attitude towards *everyone*."

(Titus 3:2) (my italics)

PRAYER

Help us, Lord, to treat everyone, whatever their race, whatever their age or appearance, as you did, with respect. And if we're the one being ill-treated, help us not to be violent, but to tell someone and be ready to forgive. Amen

VARIATIONS ON A THEME

The children could act out a series of stories from the Gospels showing how Jesus treated people equally – regardless of race, age, whatever, and how he did not meet violence with violence.

Eg. attitude to the foreigner: Matthew 8:5–13
the child: Luke 9:46–48
the disfigured: Mark 1:40–42
the bullies: Luke 22:47–51

Or you could think more about slavery in the world today, especially the forced labour of children.

(The story of John Newton in this book has more about slavery, the misery it caused and those who fought against it.)

QUIZ QUESTIONS

1. What was Belle's real first name?
2. What did her parents think might happen to her?
3. Why didn't the master sell her?
4. Later, why did she run away?
5. Being a Christian changed her attitude – how?
6. Why was she not satisfied as a maid?
7. Why did she talk to white people and not black?
8. Which president banned slavery?
9 In which state was Martin Luther King a minister?
10. What happened in Washington in 1963?

BROTHER ANDREW

Two wrongs don't make a right – taking Bibles to Communist countries

Other themes: honesty, prayer

THE PROBLEM

The boy in this story has a difficult decision to make. Listen and think what you would do.

They watched the football sailing through the air, directly on line for the Deputy Head's window. They knew what was going to happen. And there was nothing they could do to stop it.

Cra-a-ash!

They stood, all six of them, dead still. For they knew what was going to happen now too. And there was nothing they could do to stop that either.

Here he came now. Talk about angry. No-one got angry like Mr Short, the Deputy Head.

"Right!" he bellowed. "Who kicked it? I want to know now. Now!"

His words seemed to echo round the playground. But none of the six lads said anything. Mr Short glared at them one by one. He stopped at Jonathan Hill.

"You, boy! You're going red in the face. I bet it's you."

Steve, another one of the six, felt for Jonathan. He was a good mate. But Mr Short was right. It had been Jonathan who'd kicked that ball. Of course, it was an accident, pure fluke.

But Jonathan didn't say a word. He just went redder and redder.

"If it's you," snarled Mr Short, "I'm banning you from the school football team for the rest of the term."

What? Steve silently groaned in dismay. But Jonathan was the best striker!

Suddenly Mr Short turned on Steve. "You – Steven Thorpe – you're an honest lad, I know that. Tell me the truth. Did Jonathan Hill kick that ball through my window?"

Steve felt his mouth go dry. What could he say? If he said yes, that would let down his mate, and the team – they'd probably never win a match without Jonathan – so it would let down the school too. Yet saying no would be a lie.

"Well? Yes or no?"

Now think:

What would you answer? Can you see that saying no could lead to complications like the others being accused? Anyway Steve doesn't want to lie. But is "yes" the best answer?

(You could discuss this or pass on to the main story.)

THE STORY

It's hard to be completely honest when it might get us in trouble, perhaps even harder when it could hurt other people too. Here's the true story of a man who made a tough decision – and stuck to it. He's from Holland, his name is Andrew and he's known as Brother Andrew. His surname's a secret. I'll tell you why later.

Andrew loved to travel, especially to the mysterious countries behind the Iron Curtain. This was the name given to the border that separated Western Europe from the Eastern European Communist countries like Poland and Czechoslovakia.

In the fifties you couldn't easily get permission to visit these countries unless you were in a group with a guide, but Andrew was able to get away from the group to meet local Christians. He was sad to see what a hard life they had. You see, the Communist governments taught, "There is no God" and they didn't like people who disagreed.

So it could be hard for Christians to get good jobs, their churches were being closed down, and Bibles were very scarce.

As a Christian himself, Andrew wanted to help. "What do you need?" he asked.

"Above all," they answered, "we need Bibles."

Andrew could understand this as he loved the Bible himself. It gave him comfort and help, so he could imagine what God's words of love could mean to people who were suffering for their faith. But how could he get the Bibles over the border?

He managed to get a permit – called a visa – to travel by himself to Yugoslavia, another Iron Curtain country. And some old friends gave him a car, a bright blue Volkswagen, which he filled with Bibles and Bible booklets.

Andrew knew that he would be stopped at the border, knew the car could be searched. If the Bibles or booklets were found, that would be that – they would be taken away. But what if he were simply asked, "Are you carrying Bibles?" He decided then he would not lie. Jesus had called himself the Truth. So how could Andrew lie if he was following Jesus?

It was a long drive from Holland to the Yugoslav border. On the way he remembered how Jesus had made blind people see. Now Andrew wanted him to do the opposite. He prayed hard that the guards would not be able to see what he was taking to the Christians.

There was the border now. Two guards. They seemed friendly – at the moment. They looked at his passport and then inside the car.

"Let me see inside this suitcase," one said.

Andrew knew the suitcase was full of the forbidden booklets. But he had no choice. He opened it. The guard rummaged through. There they were, in the guard's own language, in full view.

But – what was happening? The guard was turning away from the suitcase, was handing Andrew back his passport, was waving him through. He'd made it. It was just as if the guard hadn't seen the booklets.

But – wasn't that just what he'd prayed?

And didn't those Yugoslav Christians welcome Andrew's gifts!

Visas came for Andrew to visit other Communist countries. As he approached each border he prayed that same prayer and God answered. The guards just couldn't seem to see the Bibles and Bible booklets.

All was going smoothly – until he went to cross the border into

Romania, a strong Communist country. His car was full of you know what. As he came near the border he knew something was wrong. The cars waiting in front of him were, one by one, being minutely examined, the guards virtually taking each car to pieces, then putting it back together, searching every piece of luggage. He'd never seen anything like it.

It wasn't just a glance in, a quick rummage. This was totally different.

As he waited in line he prayed, how he prayed. And suddenly he felt it right not to hide the Bibles better but to get some out and put them openly on the seat beside him.

After hours of waiting it was Andrew's turn. He handed the guard his passport through the window, waited to be told to get out of the car. The Bibles were quite visible.

Then – it wasn't possible – the guard handed the passport back, waved him on. Could it be happening? Was he through – just like that?

Yes, he was. Incredible. Especially when he looked back and saw them getting to work on the car behind. Everyone else – searched. But him – straight through.

Andrew realised that nothing was impossible for God.

Eventually Andrew became so well known to Communist officials that he could no longer go on such journeys. So he formed a team and trained them to go instead. That team has grown into an organisation called Open Doors.

The Iron Curtain is no more, but there are still many countries where Christians find life hard, countries like China and Cuba, so Andrew goes there now. He knows that in some places he would not be welcome – that's why he keeps his surname a secret.

He always asks the Christians what they need. They might ask for food, or clothing – one time a man asked for shoes, so Andrew gave him his own and travelled home in his socks – but usually it's Bibles that are needed.

And God goes on helping, sometimes in strange ways. Once two young women from Open Doors were asked directly at a border, "Do you have Bibles with you?"

What could they say? The car was jam-packed with them.

Suddenly their mouths were filled with laughter. "Yes!" they roared. "The car's full of Bibles!"

And the guard, thinking they were laughing at such a silly question, waved them through.

TIME OF REFLECTION

A lie, whether it is to help us or other people, can lead to big trouble. A writer called Sir Walter Scott put it this way: "O what a tangled web we weave, when first we practise to deceive." Are you honest, trustworthy? Or are you spinning tangled webs that will one day trap you?

Just take a moment to think about this.

BIBLE BITS

God is firm about lies. The Bible gives a command:

"Never say anything that isn't true. Have nothing to do with lies."

(Proverbs 4:24)

And it gives a promise:

"The Lord protects honest people."

(Proverbs 10:29)

PRAYER

Help us, Lord Jesus, to value friendship as well as truth like Steve in the first story, but help us to see, as Andrew saw, that a lie for any reason is wrong. Amen

VARIATION ON A THEME

Much of this assembly can be acted out by pupils. THE PROBLEM sketch needs an invisible football and a crash sound effect. The main story offers three sketch possibilities – the three border crossings. Chairs and a big grey blanket make a good car (though driving away would, I agree, be hard).

More details of these incidents are in Brother Andrew's books, *God's Smuggler* (Hodder and Stoughton) – Yugoslavia, chapter 10; Romania, chapter 15; and *The Calling* (Summit) – laughing, chapter 2.

"Open Doors" can be reached at PO Box 6, Witney, Oxon. OX8 7BR.

QUIZ QUESTIONS
1. Why did Andrew want to get away from his tour group in Communist countries?
2. Tell me two difficulties Christians had in those countries.
3. What did they need most of all?
4. How did Andrew get his Volkswagen?
5. Why would he not lie at the border?
6. What did he pray before every border crossing?
7. Why was it so astounding that he crossed so easily into Romania?
8. One man asked not for Bibles but for – what?
9. What is Brother Andrew's organisation called?
10. Why did the guard let the young women pass after they'd admitted having Bibles with them?

GLADYS AYLWARD

Going the extra mile – bringing God's love to China

Other themes: generosity, faith

THE PROBLEM

Listen to this. What advice would you give to the girl in this story?

The local free newspaper was on the mat when Vicky came in from school so she began to turn over the pages as she walked into the lounge. Dad, home early from work on a Friday, was asleep in the chair. Mum would be in soon with the shopping.

The paper was all ads, garden centres, restaurants, nothing that interested her. But – what was this? Suddenly she was absorbed in an article about an orphanage in a country in Eastern Europe, a country that seemed to lack every luxury and even a few necessities. A big truck was going to the orphanage from the town the next week. Readers were asked to make up packages of sweets or cheap toys to give to the children. It would be the first sweets the children would have had in a long time. Soap and toothpaste were also wanted.

"Look at this, Dad. Couldn't we give something? I was thinking about the money I got from Uncle Bob for weeding his garden, I could get a lot of sweets with that. And you could – "

"Hey, wait a minute, Vicky," said Dad, stretching. "Don't get carried away. I'm not going out and buying stuff just like that. Anyway we all put money in that charity tin last week. And you had that day at school when you needn't wear school uniform if you took 50p, and the money went to Africa, didn't it?"

"Yeah, but those things weren't my ideas, I sort of did it because it was expected. But this is my idea. I want to do it."

"No, Vicky, just forget it. You've done your bit. Let others do theirs. And just think what you could buy *yourself* with the money. You worked hard. You deserve something nice."

Vicky sighed. Yeah, she could think of lots of things she'd like to get for herself. But was it fair when she had so much and they had so little?

Now think:

Has Vicky done her bit? Shouldn't she just enjoy her hard earned money and forget about the orphanage?

(You could discuss this or pass on to the main story.)

THE STORY

Keep Vicky's idea in mind, that she wanted to do something that *she'd* thought of, not her parents or her school, while I read you this true story. It's about feet – oh, and a bloodstained axe.

Am I bowing low enough? she wondered. After all, he was the High and Mighty Mandarin of Yangcheng, the ruler of that entire district of China.

And she was just Gladys Aylward, an ordinary girl who'd become a missionary, who ran an inn in the town so she could tell the travellers stories of Jesus after the evening meal. She hadn't expected to be called into the presence of the Mandarin. What could he want? He began to speak. Gladys straightened up and listened intently.

"You know, I presume, about our ancient custom of footbinding? Baby girls have their feet tightly bound in bandages to keep them small and dainty. Now the Government has given an order. This is to stop. I imagine you know of a number of foreign women with unbound feet. Please find one who will tour the villages, making sure the new rule is known. The pay is small, but I will provide guards and a mule."

Gladys thought hard. A woman? To travel to lonely mountain villages on a mule? Who would want such a job?

But she did not speak these thoughts – the Mandarin would not listen to excuses or objections. He was the High and Mighty

Mandarin of Yangcheng.

Several weeks later she was called into his presence again. He was not pleased with Gladys's news. "What? You have found no one? Then," said the Mandarin, gazing at Gladys, "you must do it. Start tomorrow."

And that was it. Later Gladys began to see the funny side of it. How incredible! From being a simple maid in a London household to being the Mandarin's personally appointed Inspector of Feet. What a grand title! She wiggled her toes inside her size threes and laughed and laughed.

And she really enjoyed the job. It wasn't just the mountain scenery as the mule clambered up over the jagged ridges, the paths edged with wild roses, the wheat blowing in the terraced fields; it wasn't just the welcome they received from the village women pleased that the law had been changed; it was also the delight on the faces of the babies and young girls as the crippling bandages came off. Gladys would straighten the toes which were bent right back under the foot and massage them.

Then she would gather the villagers together in the square and tell them the same stories she told in the inn – Jesus stopping for water at a village well, the parable of the Sower, stories of a hard country life like their own.

One day between mule tours, she had a message from the prison governor in Yangcheng. "Come at once. A riot has broken out." So why call on me? was the question in her mind as she hurried through the streets.

The governor met her outside the entrance. "It is too dangerous for me to go in there," he said, "but you have a God who protects you. You keep telling us that. So you will be all right."

The gate was unlocked and Gladys was pushed in. She gaped at the awful sight. There were large cages round a paved courtyard. The prisoners had broken out of the cages and were attacking each other like wild animals. One was running round with a bloodstained axe, swinging it wildly.

Then they noticed her. The man with the axe started towards her. "Give me the axe!" Gladys cried out. She didn't know what to say, there'd hardly been time to think or pray. The man stopped, gazed at her, then... calmly handed her the axe.

It was as if the prisoners all came to their senses at that moment. They stood still, their heads hung in horror and shame. She saw how thin and uncared for they were. They had been treated like animals for so long, that they'd started acting like them. She talked to them. They told her they had nothing to do but sit in the cages.

The governor was thrilled she'd stopped the riot, not so thrilled when she told him sternly, "You must change the way you run the prison. You are being unfair. These men may be prisoners but they are human beings. They need things to do. They need to rebuild their lives." And she arranged for some of the prisoners to learn weaving, some to grind grain, some to breed rabbits.

Twice now Gladys had been pushed into making life better, fairer for people, first the young girls, then the prisoners.

So, later, when war broke out with Japan, and Yangcheng was bombed, and people began fleeing, she could have said, "I've done my bit. I must think of myself now." But she didn't. She collected up all the homeless children she could find and led them to safety over the mountains. There was no Mandarin or prison governor to push her into doing it. She *wanted* to do it. It was a long, long journey, most of the time on foot, through dangerous territory. But they made it.

Gladys carried on caring for those who hadn't got a fair deal in life, right up till she died in 1970. For her it was just following Jesus – hadn't *he* cared for those who hadn't had a fair deal – the lepers, the widows, the sick, the disabled? It wasn't easy for Gladys, in fact as you've heard, it was often dangerous, but when her Lord had gone all the way to the cross out of love, how could she ever say, "I've done my bit now"?

TIME OF REFLECTION

Think now: do *you* know anyone who's not had a fair deal in life? It may be someone you know personally, or you may have read about people in need, or seen them on TV. Is there anything you can do to make their lives better?

Just a moment of silence while we think about this.

BIBLE BITS

Listen to what the Bible says:

Jesus said: "Love one another. As I have loved you, so you must love one another." (John 13:34)

"Help to carry one another's burdens, and in this way you will obey the law of Christ." (Galatians 6:2)

"The Lord Jesus himself said, 'There is more happiness in giving than in receiving.'" (Acts 20:35)

PRAYER

Father God, I have so much to eat and drink, I have so much fun and enjoyment. Give me eyes to see people in need so I can make things a bit fairer by sharing what I have. Help me to do it because I want to, not because I have to. Amen

VARIATIONS ON THE THEME

Pupils could bring in stories cut from newspapers and magazines to show the variety of needs in the world. Contrasts could be made with the abundance we have. The assembly could lead into a charity support idea, but to fit in with the stories here, the initiative should come from the children.

Or pupils could perform the story of the Good Samaritan (Luke 10), or invent short plays based on the "more happiness in giving" verse above.

QUIZ QUESTIONS

1. What had been Gladys's job back in England?
2. Why had the Mandarin called Gladys into his presence?
3. What size shoe did she take?
4. What sort of Bible story did she tell the village people?
5. Why did the Governor ask her to stop the riot?
6. One of the prisoners handed her something – what?
7. What was wrong with the way the prison was being run?
8. How did Gladys help the prisoners rebuild their lives?
9. Why was it necessary to take the children away from Yangcheng?
10. Why did she do so much for needy people?

GEORGE MULLER

The hope that God answers prayer – children's homes in Bristol

Other themes: God as Father, faith

THE PROBLEM

Listen to this and see if you agree with what's said at the end.

Class 5P settled back into the classroom after the vicar's assembly. The teacher was sorting out some books, so Sean turned to the others on his table.

"Do you believe all that stuff he said about prayer?"

"Dunno," said Lisa. "Be good if it worked. Like rubbing a magic lamp and making a wish."

Jenny just shrugged her shoulders.

"Look," Sean said, grinning, "why don't we all pray for something over this weekend? Then we'll know if it works. I'm gonna pray my dad wins the National Lottery."

Lisa giggled. "Ooh, remember I'm your friend! I'll pray... let's see... for a distinction in my piano exam. What about you, Jenny?"

Jenny thought. "Well... my Gran's in hospital. I'm going to pray that she's a lot better by the time we visit on Sunday."

Monday morning. Class 5P shuffled in.

"Well?" said Lisa.

"You must be joking," said Sean. "Nowhere near. Not a single number."

"I know how you feel," said Lisa. "I didn't get my distinction either. What about your Gran, Jenny?"

"Well," she began, "Gran was more cheerful than usual, and that was nice, but she wasn't any better really, no."

"So," proclaimed Sean. "We've proved it. Prayer doesn't work. Shame really."

Now think:

Have they really proved that prayer doesn't work? Did any of the prayers make a difference? Do you agree with Lisa that prayer is like rubbing a magic lamp and making a wish?

(You could discuss this or pass on to the main story.)

THE STORY

Here's a true story about a man who prayed – but not to win the National Lottery!

The police officer looked very serious. "Mr Muller, I regret to inform you that your son George has been arrested for robbery."

Mr Muller groaned. "Oh no... but he's only sixteen."

Yet he could well believe it. George had been trouble from the beginning – lying, stealing, cheating. Mr Muller had punished him hard and often but it had made no difference. And he'd so hoped that George would become a respectable citizen, maybe even a man of the church. But now – jail! Would he ever change?

But four years later, in 1825, George did change. A friend invited him to a meeting of Christians in someone's home. And George heard someone pray, not just say a prayer, but really pray. Wow, he thought, you can really talk to God – just like a child talks to his father. And God hears – *and* answers. What a Father to have!

George understood for the first time that being a Christian wasn't just following a set of rules, but a relationship with a powerful God, and that it wasn't boring – it was an adventure!

He said yes to God straight away, and over the next years learnt he could trust God for everything he needed. So that when he got a job, in charge of a church in Teignmouth in Devon, instead of taking a salary, he just prayed that God would provide all his needs. And it worked. No, the food didn't drop out of the sky, but God told other Christians, "Take one of your pies round to George", or "Your pastor needs a new pair of shoes."

Later George moved to the great city of Bristol to look after a church there, again trusting God to give him all he needed.

Bristol was very different to Teignmouth. The streets were teeming with orphans. Perhaps the parents had been killed by disease, leaving the kids to fend for themselves. These kids ended up in workhouses and prisons. Or they became beggars and thieves, roaming the streets at night like wild animals. Or they just crept into dark alleys to die.

George pleaded with God for them. "Father, please do something for these children."

And God spoke to George's heart. "George, I long to help them. But I need you to work with me. I want you to open a home for these children where they can grow up safe and loved. And I promise I will provide everything that's needed."

A children's home? Could God do it? Of course he could, thought George, for he's God – and he will, for he loves these kids as much as he loves me.

George was also thrilled that people would see God at work and begin to trust him more in their own lives.

So he began praying for the right house and the right staff. He told people what he was planning but he never asked any person for money or help, only God. And God put it in people's hearts to give and offer their services. Less than four months later, in May 1836, the orphan home for thirty girls was up and running.

But George did not stop there. Nor did God. In the next years three more homes were opened, one for babies, one for older boys, and another for girls. No one had been asked for a penny, only God.

And it will continue that way, George decided. They would just pray, for money to pay the staff, for all the food and everything else needed.

Sometimes it would come in the nick of time. The milkman or the baker would be on their way to collect their money and there wouldn't be a penny to pay them. But someone would always get there just in time with a donation, saying, "God's just told me to come round with this money", or something like that.

It wasn't long before the four little houses became very cramped – there were 130 living in them after all! So George prayed about moving. To a big house. A very big house. Again George asked no one but God for the money. But in it came, and in July 1847, building began on a house for no less than three hundred orphans.

God's next move would have knocked out a lesser man than George. For God said, "I want you to build another orphanage. Next door to this one. A bigger one."

A colossal amount of money would be involved. A fortune. Ah, thought George, but God is a colossal God. He can do it. And in November 1857 a home for four hundred children was opened.

Even that wasn't the end. Number three orphanage was built across the road, and numbers four and five round the corner.

George Muller made a huge difference to the lives of thousands of orphan children. But George would have said, "It was God who did it. I just prayed."

George died in 1898. But the work is still going today, helping not just children, but whole families, through day centres, or visits to their homes, or by working with local churches.

And there's still the belief that prayer works. If it didn't work, I reckon they'd have stopped by now, don't you?

TIME OF REFLECTION

Let me ask you: have you ever really prayed? Not just said prayers without thinking about them, not just said Amen at the end of someone else's because it's the thing to do, but really prayed? It worked for George Muller. Do you think it would work for you?

A moment of silence to think about that.

BIBLE BITS

The Bible says that prayer should be serious and sincere:

"When you pray, go to your room, close the door, and pray to your Father, who is unseen. And your Father . . will reward you."
(Matthew 6:6)

"The prayer of a good person has a powerful effect."
(James 5:16)

PRAYER

Father, thank you that you want to give us your best – and that you want us to ask for it. But help us to understand too that prayer is not like reading out a shopping list, but part of a relationship with a loving, generous God. Amen

VARIATIONS ON A THEME

The first story would be effective acted out.

Or pupils could read out prayers you have written ("Please may I come top in the exam?"; "Please make their best player fall ill so our team can win the match for once."; "Help me be more patient with my little brother." And so on.) The audience could say if they think God is likely to answer the prayer with a yes. Help them understand that prayer is part of a relationship rather than another way of getting what we want.

More information on the work of the George Muller Foundation and details of school tours of its museum can be obtained from Mr Julian Marsh, Chief Executive, The George Muller Foundation, 7 Cotham Park, Bristol BS6 6DA

QUIZ QUESTIONS

1. How old was George Muller when he was arrested for robbery?
2. What did George find so surprising at the first Christian meeting he went to?
3. From that time George thought of God as HIS – what?
4. What shocked him about Bristol?
5. When money was needed, George asked – who?
6. Why did they move from the four small houses?
7. How many orphans could live in the first big house?
8. Where was the next orphanage built?
9. And how many could live there?
10. Did George have a big bank balance?

PATRICIA ST JOHN

The hope of God's encouragement – nursing in Morocco

Other themes: perseverance, feelings of failure

THE PROBLEM

Listen to this. What would you do in this situation?

The letters arrived just before going home time. Sarah opened hers quickly. The words jumped out at her: "I am sorry to tell you that you have failed your Cycling Proficiency Test. The points you failed on are listed – " But then her eyes prickled with tears and it all went blurred.

Failed? But she... never failed at things. And she needed to pass the test, otherwise she couldn't ride her bike to school. She jammed her eyes shut to keep the tears hidden.

She could still hear though. Around her the class was in uproar: "Look, I passed" – "Great, so did I" – "Phew, made it". The noise seemed to be pressing down on her. Suddenly there was a quiet voice right by her ear. "Don't worry, Sarah, you're not the only one." It was her teacher, Mrs Wilson, trying to be nice. "Dan didn't pass, nor did Tina or Jonathan. And you can always take the test again."

Yeah, she felt like saying, but they're used to failing. It's not the same for me. And as for taking it again, never, not ever. Her father would just have to keep bringing her to school, that was all there was to it.

Then there was another voice. Jackie, her best friend. "Didn't fail, did you? Aah, hard luck."

Sarah blinked her eyes open and managed a smile. "Aw, who cares?" But deep inside she felt hurt and sad.

Now think:
Should Sarah put this behind her and concentrate on the things she's good at, the things she's bound to succeed at? Or should she try again? Why doesn't she want to take the test again, do you think?

(You could discuss this or pass on to the main story.)

THE STORY

Now a true story about someone who faced failure. Her name is Patricia St John.

Patricia guessed it could be the end of her nursing career when she saw the cat. There it sat, pleased to have found a place in the warm, not realising that it was the very place it shouldn't be – on a trolley spread with medical equipment ready to be used in the hospital. Now it would all have to be sterilised again. What would Matron say about that?

And just because she'd left the door open. Of course, she could make the excuse it was war-time and she was rushed off her feet with all the bomb victims coming in. But it was her fault and she knew it.

So did Matron. "Do you think, Patricia, it might be better if you did something other than nursing? And look at your health record – you've been off sick so often. You've a good brain, there are other jobs you could do."

Patricia decided to go for a long walk to make the decision – to keep going or to give up. As she walked she remembered how God had guided her into nursing – it was 1943 and the country needed nurses so much – and how she had felt him helping her during the three months of training.

But now she was on the wards, it didn't seem to be working out. The problem was she was so afraid of making mistakes – and of Matron seeing them, so afraid of being a failure. And these fears were making her ill. Really, for her own sake, for other people's sake, it would be better...

Then she saw it. A huge hoarding outside a railway station with a Bible verse in big black letters: "Jesus said, 'Do you believe that

I am able to do this?'" She knew it was God speaking to her. He was saying, "Do you believe I am able to help you in your work, give you all the help you need, or do you, Patricia, believe I made a mistake when I chose this job for you?"

And then and there, Patricia accepted not only God's help, but also the fact that the occasional failing at this or that or forgetting this or that was not the end of the world. God could give her the confidence to keep going.

And she went back on the wards with a different attitude – no longer living in fear of Matron, but able to accept that she was still learning, that she wouldn't, couldn't, get everything right, make everyone better, or stop the war. But she could do what God sent her there to do. And after that day, she had no more time off sick. She felt great.

And she was willing to try new things. When the war was over she became a housemother in a boarding school, and, wanting a suitable book to read to children made unhappy by war, she decided to write it herself. You can still get it today, it's called *The Tanglewoods' Secret*. It's even been made into a film.

Then her brother, who was in charge of a hospital in Morocco in North Africa, wrote to her: "There's so much work out here. Can you come and help?"

So she went.

It was hard work though, very hard. It was a new country, a new language, a whole new way of doing things. But Patricia kept at it, communicating at first with just hands and eyebrows, pushing away the feelings of homesickness that threatened to wash over her.

Then she went on to do something even more difficult – to open and run a clinic in a little Moroccan mountain town. It was a lonely job – no one else spoke English and many were suspicious of her: "Who is she?", "What's she here for?"

But she kept on doing her best, and bit by bit the townspeople came to accept and love her. They even brought their animals to her – mules with sores on their backs would be squeezed protesting through the door of the tiny clinic. The tricky bit was pushing the mules back out again after treatment!

On particularly hard days there would come the feeling of

failure and the temptation to give up and go home. Then one day Patricia was walking back from a distant village when she saw a woman hurrying down a hillside calling to her. "The English nurse?" she asked.

"Yes."

The woman uncovered a bundle she held in her arms. It was a baby with infected eyes, its swollen eyelids stuck together. The woman told Patricia, "Last night I had a dream. Someone in white told me to take my baby to the English nurse on the main road at this time." She did not know Patricia, could not have known she would be passing that spot at that time. Except that God had told her in her dream. For God knew Patricia had just the right treatment for the baby.

And Patricia felt happy, for she knew that she was doing what God had planned for her to do. If she had given up, what would have happened to that baby and the hundreds of other babies and children and adults she treated? Oh – and the mules, mustn't forget those.

Patricia St John died in 1993, still caring for the poor of the world. And her stories – there are several set in Morocco – are still read and enjoyed today.

TIME OF REFLECTION

I'd like you to think what you want to do this year, what you want to achieve. I'm not talking about impossible things, but maybe learning a new skill, or doing better at something, reaching the next level. What if it isn't so easy, what if it doesn't seem to be working out straight away – will you give up? Are you willing to fail before you succeed? If you believe in God, what difference will that make?

Just a moment of silence while we think about these things.

BIBLE BITS

Listen to what the Bible says:

"Be determined and confident! Don't be afraid or discouraged, for I, the Lord your God, am with you wherever you go."

(Joshua 1:9)

"Let us run with determination the race that lies before us. Let us keep our eyes fixed on Jesus ... He did not give up ..."

(Hebrews 12:1–2)

PRAYER

Thank you, Father, that you have given me the ability to succeed, not in everything, but in many things. Help me to play my part by working hard and not giving up. And thank you that you will give me extra help if I ask for it and trust in you. May what I learn not just help me but others too. Amen

VARIATION ON A THEME

The main story could be mimed by children as you read. Matron, brother, villagers and woman with baby could be speaking parts using the words in the story.

QUIZ QUESTIONS

1. Why was Patricia worried when she saw the cat on the trolley?
2. What was making Patricia ill?
3. Why were nurses needed so much at that time?
4. What did the Bible verse on the hoarding say?
5. Why did she write *The Tanglewoods' Secret*?
6. Where was her brother working?
7. Then she went to a mountain town. What for?
8. Why were mules brought to Patricia?
9. What message did the woman get in her dream?
10. Why was meeting the woman such an encouragement to Patricia?

MICHAEL FARADAY

The hope that God rewards patience – working with electricity

Other themes: rumours, not jumping to conclusions

THE PROBLEM

Listen and think what you would do if you were in this situation.

Lucy stretched one arm out of bed. Good that today was Saturday – no school. She was tired.

Well, it *had* been a great birthday party, everyone said so. It was good of Mum and Dad to get all those pizzas in and not moan when they turned the volume up on the CD player.

Just a shame Helen hadn't been able to come. They'd been friends for ages, but just recently Helen had been a bit quiet. She'd rung up just an hour before the party to say that she felt sick and she wouldn't be coming, sorry and all that.

Lucy finally got herself out of bed and had just got downstairs when the phone rang. "I'll get it," she shouted. Could be Helen, she thought.

But it was Emma. "Hi, Lucy. Listen, I thought you said Helen was sick. Well, I saw her on the way home from the party last night, coming out of the cinema she was, with some other people. I only glimpsed her out of the car window, but I'm fairly sure it was her."

Lucy felt hurt, then angry. When Emma had rung off, she began dialling Helen's number, her fingers trembling a little. Then she banged it down. No, I'll write her a letter, she thought. That way she can't interrupt. My brother can take it round on his bike. Best friend – huh. Best liar, more like.

Or... perhaps... She looked at the phone again.

Now think:
What should she do? What mistake is she making? What could be the result?

(You could discuss this or pass on to the main story.)

THE STORY

Our true story is about a man who, unlike Lucy, didn't jump to conclusions. He was born in 1791 but his inventions are still being used today. In fact *you've* used one today. All of you have.

Michael Faraday stared in puzzlement at his workbench, at his equipment, at his notes. Why wasn't the experiment working? He really believed electricity, used together with magnetism, could make things move. But until he'd proved it, it was only a theory, an idea.

And what use was a theory? Oh yes, he could do what many scientists did and publish his ideas, and people would say, "Brilliant, brilliant. What a splendid fellow Faraday is." But that wasn't what he wanted. He just wanted to be sure he was right. So he had to prove it.

And he believed one day he would. He would not give up hope. He felt God would reward his patience. One day.

He turned to look round his laboratory. The hundreds of little bottles lining the shelves winked at him as the sunlight fell on them. "Go on, discover *our* secrets," they seemed to be challenging him. "With God's help, I will," he murmured. "In time. Now let's try this one again. I'll try it like this. Now let's see..."

This fascination with science had begun in Mr Riebau's bookshop where he had been an apprentice bookbinder. He loved dipping into the books customers brought in for binding. Anything on chemistry or electricity would hold him spellbound – until Mr Riebau called out, "You're here to bind 'em, not read 'em, Michael."

But Michael knew there'd be a smile on his employer's face. Mr Riebau was like a second father to him, having hired him first as a delivery boy when he was thirteen. When he saw how hardworking he was, a year later he offered him a free apprenticeship. His future was as secure as it could be.

But for Michael the world of leather bindings was too safe. It was the world of science that excited him, its experiments and explosions, its dangers and discoveries. He went to scientific lectures and came out his head bursting with questions and ideas: "What if – this? What if – that?" Michael longed to be a scientist himself and answer all those "what if" questions himself.

The most exciting lectures were given by Sir Humphry Davy. Michael wrote up his notes after each of his lectures in beautiful handwriting, bound them into a book, then sent it to Sir Humphry asking if he could have a job working for him. It was a chance in a million, like one of you writing to a chart-topping group and asking to join.

But for Michael it worked. Just after the book arrived, one of Sir Humphry's assistants got the sack for fighting, and he was in. Michael must have said "Wow!" a hundred times – or whatever they said in 1813.

He probably also said "Thank you". Because Michael would have known someone was guiding and helping him. God. Michael had been a faithful member of his little church near St. Paul's Cathedral since he was young.

And God had another surprise in store. Sir Humphry decided to take a trip abroad to meet top European scientists. He would take with him his wife – and his new assistant. A few more "Wows".

It wasn't two lazy weeks in the sun though. It was eighteen months and not always easy. Sir Humphry's wife loved bossing Michael about, and he missed English food.

But he got to meet scientists like Ampere and Volta – who gave their names to ways of measuring electricity – amperes, or amps, and volts. So you can guess what subject they talked about!

Back home Michael plunged into all kinds of experiments. He knew that God had given him a real talent, and didn't want to let him down. He experimented with sugar and seaweed, stainless steel and heatproof glass, discovering things which made life better and safer.

But it was electricity which fascinated him most. No one really used electricity in those days. Even Ampere and Volta couldn't see how it could change the world.

Michael Faraday could. But he made a decision to say nothing about his ideas for the time being. Weeks, months, years went by. Faraday sat, thinking, experimenting, refusing to jump to conclusions, for that could just confuse people; no! – more than confuse them – wrong conclusions could hurt people: he had to make sure his ideas were safe.

And then it happened: magnets like this, batteries connected like this, and, yes, that wire was moving! Nothing had exploded, no one been electrocuted. But something had moved! Moved through the power of electricity!

He checked the results. Yes!

He rechecked. Yes again!

Faraday was sure of his ground now. Now he could speak out.

By 1862 he had recorded over 16,000 experiments. But by then he had invented his Big Three – the electric motor, the transformer and the dynamo. Dozens of inventions depend on one or more of these Big Three. Turned on a light? Been in a car? Played a cassette? Made yourself some toast?

Be glad then for a man who didn't jump to conclusions. He sat and thought and he checked his facts. That's how he got it right.

TIME OF REFLECTION

Not just in science, but in our daily lives too, jumping to conclusions can get us in a mess. It can hurt other people too, if we accuse them unfairly or, perhaps worse, if we spread rumours about them. Have you ever opened your mouth before you should, before you'd really checked out the facts?

Just take a moment to think about this.

BIBLE BITS

The Bible tells us to play it cool:

"Good people think before they answer."

(Proverbs 15:28)

"Thoughtless words can wound as deeply as any sword."
(Proverbs 12:18)

"Everyone must be quick to listen, but slow to speak and slow to become angry."
(James 1:19)

PRAYER

Help us, Lord, to be slow to speak – to check on the facts before we accuse someone or before we make a decision. And help us not to be gossips or rumour spreaders – ever. Amen

VARIATION ON A THEME

Explain the Big Three inventions (motor, transformer, dynamo), then ask children to suggest ways life would be different without them. Use an OHP to make a list.

QUIZ QUESTIONS

1. How old was Michael when Mr Riebau first employed him?
2. How did he first get interested in science?
3. What did he send to Sir Humphry Davy?
4. He'd have thanked Sir Humphry for the job – who else?
5. How long was the trip abroad?
6. What would he have talked about with Ampere and Volta?
7. Why did he want to check out all his ideas?
8. Can you name one of his Big Three inventions?
9. And another?
10. And another?

ESTHER JOHN

The hope that God's Word is true – the cost of commitment in Pakistan

Other themes: RE lessons, Easter story, death

THE PROBLEM

Listen to this and see what you think.

Monday morning after assembly. There was a buzz of excitement in Mr Turner's class, for the timetable of the week's lessons was being given out. There were always a few moans if the word "fractions" appeared, and noises of approval if the science involved experiments – they could be fun.

But it was the RE which the group at the corner table were discussing.

"'A Look at the Bible, week 1'," groaned James. "But I don't wanna look at it. It's just stories from thousands of years ago. Just made up stuff. Boring, boring, boring."

"You're stupid," said Amy. "They're lovely stories. Doesn't matter if they're made up, they're lovely."

Craig shook his head. "Well, I don't know if it's true, I don't know much about the Bible at all. But I'll listen to what Mr Turner says, and perhaps have a go at reading it myself. Then I'll tell you my opinion."

Now think:

What do you think about what each of them said? Is the Bible just old stories? Does it matter if they're true or not? What about what Craig said? Who's going to get the most out of the lessons?

(You could discuss this or pass on to the main story.)

THE STORY

(You may wish to omit or modify the introduction to the story which follows – but the quiz at the end is based on the information in it!)

I don't know what you believe about the Bible, but most Christians believe that the writers were helped by God so that everything in it is just as God wants it. God used about 40 different people to write the 66 books that make up the Bible, that's 39 books in the Old Testament, 27 in the New.

The Bible teaches us about God, what he's like, and how he was born on earth as a human being, Jesus. The story of Jesus is told in the Gospels – Matthew, Mark, Luke and John.

The Bible's about us too, how we should live, how we should pray, how we should treat other people, and how God can be our friend for ever.

So it's a lot more than a book of old stories!

I want to tell you about a girl called Qamar Zia who believed the Bible to be a very special book indeed. The end of the story is not what you'd expect.

Let's go to the other side of the world – to India.

Qamar looked suspiciously at the book on her desk. She wanted nothing to do with it. "Why did my parents send me to this school?" she moaned to herself. "I don't want to study this strange religion."

But now the teacher was telling the class to open the book at a certain page. Reluctantly Qamar touched the cover, flipped it open. "Qamar," she told herself, "don't be silly. You are seventeen years old, not a baby. What can a book do to you?" Sighing she turned to the right page.

And so, for the first time, Qamar Zia began to study the Bible. Well, sort of study it. Much of the time, her mind was not on it. The sultry heat of the Indian summer seemed to seep into every corner of the classroom, and every corner of her brain too.

Until one day when everything changed. One moment the words, oh such difficult words, were swimming hazily before her eyes, the next they seemed to be alive, the most important words in the world. The chapter was in the Old Testament, Isaiah chapter 53.

"Like a lamb about to be slaughtered,
like a sheep about to be sheared,
he never said a word.
He was arrested and sentenced and led off to die ..."

Qamar knew who this was about: Jesus.

"... he endured the suffering that should have been ours.
... because of our sins he was wounded, beaten because of the evil we did."

Qamar's heart was thumping. This Jesus – he'd died... for her? Taken punishment... for her? She read on.

"... his death was a sacrifice to bring forgiveness."

Forgiveness... for her? Before, she'd believed that it was enough to live a good life, but deep down she knew she was not good enough and needed forgiveness.

And this Jesus, she suddenly remembered, had come back to life after this terrible death. Was he alive now? How could it be?

Over the next days she could think of little else and gradually it sank in. Jesus was real, he loved her, he had died for her, he wanted to be her friend and companion for ever. And Qamar said yes. How could she turn away from such a friend?

But she told no one at home, for in her family becoming a Christian was not acceptable. They would be very angry if they found out.

Qamar was not to stay in that school for long for it was 1947 and what had been part of northern India was now to become a separate country, Pakistan, and her family wanted to be part of it.

It was a difficult time: a long journey to a strange land, having to live in temporary accommodation, thousands of people around her all wondering what the future would hold. And Qamar had no Bible to read.

But one day she had a visitor, a Christian woman working nearby. "Your old school told me you were here. Can I help in any way?"

Qamar nodded. "Oh yes. A New Testament, please. But if my family knew..."

So, a few days later, a New Testament was passed to her inside a larger book. And for the next seven years Qamar kept it hidden.

Then what she feared happened. No, they didn't find the book. Worse in a way. Her parents began to arrange her marriage – to a man she didn't love, a man who would try to stop her believing in Jesus.

She pleaded with her mother. It grew into an argument and ended with Qamar leaving home. She went to stay at the orphanage where the Christian woman worked. Perhaps in time, she thought, they will understand how good Jesus is, perhaps in time I will be able to live at home as a Christian.

But meanwhile how good it was to study the Bible with others again – she had so many questions – and how enjoyable to help look after the orphan children. She was given a new name while she was there – Esther John: Esther, a beautiful and brave queen in the Old Testament; John, the disciple who was closest to Jesus. She had never been happier.

Then came another shock. "You are to be marrried straight away," her family told her. She knew she would be forced to go through with it. She had to get right away. She fled to the north of the country and became a nurses' helper in a hospital.

But it was teaching, not nursing, that she had her heart set on. Teaching the Bible. So she entered a special school for training.

Her training completed, she went to a little town called Chichawatni to live and work with an older couple, Mr and Mrs White. Esther loved cycling to the villages around with Mrs White. It was quite an adventure. When they arrived in a village, Esther would play the dholki, a kind of drum, and people would gather round to hear about a village carpenter who was God, the one who was "led out to die" to bring forgiveness. And Esther often found time to help the village women with their babies or by picking cotton in the fields.

Then a letter came. From her family. "Your youngest brother is to get married. Please come and live at home. Your mother needs you."

Esther prayed and wrote back: "I will come if I can live as a Christian and not be forced into marriage."

There was no answer.

The weeks went by. Then one morning Esther did not come to breakfast. The Whites called to her. But Esther could not hear.

For during the night someone had got into her room and killed her.

Who? Why?

The police found no clues. No one was ever arrested. There were some people who felt it was wrong for her to turn from the family religion and believe in Jesus, but who knows? It's a mystery. A mystery too why God allowed such a terrible, sad thing to happen.

But in one way it was not so sad for Esther herself. For she believed in the Bible, a book in which Jesus had promised, when the time was right, to take her to her home in heaven to be close to him for ever.

In 1998 ten statues were put up on the outside of Westminster Abbey in London. They are statues of people who have died because they followed Jesus. One of the statues is of Esther John.

TIME OF REFLECTION

Esther believed the Bible so strongly that she could not give it up. But why exactly did she love it? How would you complete this sentence – "Esther John loved the Bible because…"? Just take a moment to think about that.

BIBLE BITS

One of the Bible writers said:

"How sweet is the taste of your instructions – sweeter even than honey!

I obey your teachings; I love them with all my heart.

Your word is a lamp to guide me and a light for my path."
(Psalm 119:103,167,105)

But the only way you'll know if he was wise is by getting to know the Bible for yourself!

PRAYER

Father, thank you for the Bible, what it meant to Esther John and what it can mean to us. But help us to remember that you don't want us to worship a book, but the person the book's about, Jesus. Amen

VARIATIONS ON A THEME

Pupils may like to read a favourite Bible verse or story and say why it is special to them.

Or they may enjoy selecting an additional name for themselves from the Bible, thinking about which character they most resemble or would most like to resemble – other than Jesus.

The source of the information on Esther John is the chapter on her life by Dr Patrick Sookhdeo in *The Terrible Alternative*, ed. Andrew Chandler, published by Cassell, 1998. More information about Pakistan, etc can be obtained by writing to The Barnabas Fund, The Old Rectory, River Street, Pewsey, Wiltshire SN9 5DB

QUIZ QUESTIONS

(Based mainly on the information at the beginning of THE STORY section)

1. The Bible is like a library. How many separate books are there in it?
2. It's divided into two parts called – ?
3. How many books are there in the Old Testament?
4. How many books are there in the New Testament?
5. The books were written by – about how many different authors?
6. The four Gospels tell us about Jesus' life. Name one.
7. And another.
8. And another.
9. And another.
10. Which Bible book spoke to Esther's heart?

GAVIN PEACOCK / BERNHARD LANGER / JONATHAN EDWARDS

The hope that life is more than failure or success – football, golf, athletics

Other themes: coping with disappointment, taking sport too seriously

THE PROBLEM

Listen to this and see what you think at the end.

Karen could hear part of the crowd chanting her name: "Ka-ren! Ka-ren!" They knew it all depended on her – she knew it too. If she won this final race in the Inter-School Swimming Gala, Compton, her school, would carry away the trophy. It would be tight though: Compton and one of the rival schools, The Laurels, had equal points. It was up to her.

But she was confident. The swimmer for The Laurels looked nervous. Winning shouldn't be too much of a problem.

And the gun went off. She dived. Good, long, clean strokes, come on!

But on the second lap, she began to feel tired for some reason. Push, Karen told herself, push! She was vaguely aware of the roaring crowd, vaguely aware too that she was not in the lead. Push! Push!

Then it was over. And there was the girl from The Laurels jumping about in the water. She'd won. Karen was, what, fourth, maybe even fifth. She pulled herself out of the pool, trying to keep from crying until she was alone. Behind her as she ran, she heard a teacher saying, "Bad luck, Karen, but stay around, we're about to take team photos."

But Karen didn't stop. Not until she reached the changing room where she buried her head in her towel and let the sobs come. She felt so ashamed. She'd done her best, but she'd let everyone down.

Then she heard a voice, "Karen, the photo, come on... "

Now think:
What should she do? Is she right to be ashamed? What would you say to her?

(You could discuss this or pass on to the main story.)

THE STORY

Picture the scene. Wembley Stadium. You're there in the crowd – and it's the FA Cup Final, 1994, Chelsea versus Manchester United. The teams haven't come onto the pitch yet, but you can feel the excitement all around you. The atmosphere's electric.

Ah, here they come, striding onto the turf, Chelsea in blue, Man United in red. They look tiny in the vast stadium, but you know they're giants of the game. Even so, this is one of the biggest days of their lives, they've worked so hard to get here. If you're excited, how must they feel?

The game begins. The minutes tick by. No score yet. They're playing their hearts out but the break hasn't come to either side.

Then it happens. A chance. Gavin Peacock for Chelsea has the ball, outside the box, but there's not much between him and the goal. He shifts the ball from the right foot to the left, not much time now before the Reds pour down. He kicks. Yes – it looks dead on line for the goal, the ball flying through the air, unstoppable surely. The crowd holds its breath. It's nearly there...

Oh no! It's hit the crossbar, bounced out!

If it had gone in, Chelsea would have been in the lead, they'd have been able to put ten men in defence and just hold on to win. Ah, if only ...

But how does Gavin Peacock himself feel about it? We'll hear later.

Let's change the scene. 1991, a golf course in the United States.

Two teams, Europe and the States, playing for the Ryder Cup. A big, big match. And now the result hangs on one short putt. If the German Bernhard Langer knocks it in, Europe wins. If he misses, it's a win for the States.

The ball's only lying about two metres from the hole and Langer is very experienced, very cool. He takes a couple of practice strokes and moves to the correct position. He looks at the ball, the hole, back to the ball again. The spectators are like statues.

And, click, the ball begins to roll towards the hole, closer, closer, it's right at the edge now. But – it doesn't go in, it just slides round the rim of the hole and comes to rest a short distance away. He's missed.

The US team jump and dance about. And Bernhard Langer – do you think he does the same?

Yes, how did these sportsmen feel? After that kick did Gavin Peacock mentally give up? After that shot did Langer throw his putter on the ground in rage?

In a word, no. Gavin Peacock knows that was just one kick. He did his best at that moment. All right, it didn't work out. But he can live with it, he can carry on with the game, continue doing his best.

For he knows that one of the most valuable assets in professional football is a level head, whatever comes. He knows that one moment the crowd could be roaring out his name, the next he could be out of the team. Being a Christian helps him cope with failure and success and not get too worked up about either. He knows God's given him a terrific talent as a striker, but he knows too that God hasn't promised he'll get every ball in. He's just promised to be with him in the good moments and the bad, with him always.

Gavin comes from a footballing family. When he was small, his dad, who was a Charlton player for seventeen years, used to place balls round the garden so Gavin would get in the habit of kicking them. Eventually he went in for the England schoolboy trials, got in the team and played at Wembley when he was fifteen – in fact he played at Wembley on the Saturday and took his Maths GCE on the Monday.

He became a professional as soon as he left school, playing for Queens Park Rangers and Newcastle before Chelsea. Then he moved back to Queens Park Rangers.

Gavin always prays about which club to join and he feels God guiding him. And he prays for strength too – both in his legs and in his mind when things aren't going so well. But he knows there's more to life than football, much more.

Bernhard Langer, the golfer, says the same. Knowing that his talent comes from God, and knowing Jesus as a friend standing by him, even when he misses, helps him a lot. Of course, he was sad to let his team down in that Ryder Cup, but his responsibility is to do his best, not to make every shot, win every tournament. What he says is, "There has only ever been one perfect human being, and we crucified him – I only missed a putt."

Anyway winning has its problems too. In the World Athletics Championships in Sweden in 1995, Jonathan Edwards broke the world record for the triple jump – 18 metres 16, a fantastic distance. But then he jumped again – and broke the record again – 18 metres 29 this time. He knew he'd done well, but when he realised just how well, he gave one of the biggest grins ever seen on a human face. Then to top that he won the BBC Sports Personality Award for that year.

It must be hard to be modest after that. In fact it must be easy to think you're the king of the world. But Jonathan doesn't think that way. He says he's no more important than the person who measured those jumps. They just have different jobs, different talents.

For, like the others, Jonathan is a Christian and he knows his ability comes from God. But he knows too the danger of making sport the only thing in your life – you can overtrain, get boastful or tense – you can stop enjoying sport if you take it too seriously. In the end he knows there's got to be something more important than jumping into a sandpit.

So – you won, you're the champion? You're not the king of the world – don't act like it.

You lost? So? It's not the end of the world. God loves you, winner or loser. Doesn't *that* have to be the most important thing?

TIME OF REFLECTION

Yes, we know winning's best, but – what do you think? – perhaps we need to experience a bit of both, winning and losing. And I'm not just talking about sport here, but about any competition we go in for. Now we know what we can gain by winning, a medal, a feeling of achievement and so on, but I want you to think what you can gain by losing. Just a moment to think about that...

Well, what did you think of? Perhaps that losing can make you try harder, make you more determined. Perhaps that it can make you more sympathetic, so you can encourage others when they lose.

So perhaps losing can be winning too. We need to learn how to do both.

BIBLE BITS

Be careful if you win a lot. The Bible says:

"Too much honey is bad for you."

(Proverbs 25:27)

and "Do not think of yourself more highly than you should."

(Romans 12:3)

And if you keep on losing, there's this verse:

"If we do not give up, the time will come when we will reap the harvest."

(Galatians 6:9)

PRAYER

Lord, help us to be good losers and good winners, to do our best and leave it there whatever the result. You know we're not Superman or Superwoman, but thank you for the abilities that you have given us. Amen

VARIATION ON A THEME

Pupils could speak about sports events or other competitions they entered, and, even though they didn't win, how much they enjoyed them anyway. This would show that the result is not the be-all and end-all and that losing is nothing to be ashamed of.

QUIZ QUESTIONS

1. Which teams played in the 1994 FA Cup Final?
2. What stopped that ball Gavin Peacock kicked from going in?
3. What was Gavin's reaction?
4. How did Gavin's dad get him in the habit of kicking balls?
5. What did Gavin do on the Saturday before his Maths GCE?
6. Tell me one thing Gavin always prays about.
7. Which country is Bernhard Langer from?
8. Name the golfing cup the teams were playing for.
9. Which event is Jonathan Edwards famous for?
10. What did he do in Sweden that was so special?

WILLIAM CAREY

The hope that God can be a personal friend – Bible translation in India

Other themes: special places, "quiet times"

THE PROBLEM

Listen to this and see what you think.

Peter loved the beach. It was his special place. The place he went to when he wanted to be alone and quiet for a bit. You see, his three younger brothers didn't know the meaning of the word "quiet" – their whole lives seemed to be given over to shouting, screaming, bawling and giggling. So he came down to the beach, to his own special sand dune. Only his mum knew where it was.

He'd scoop out a hollow in the sand to sit in and lean back against the dune. He'd buried a plastic bag of his stuff there – his latest reading book, a book of children's prayers which cheered him up when he was low, a pocket game, and some sweets. He'd dig up his treasure and sit back. Apart from the breeze in the wild grass, it was silent. Ah, peace at last.

Then one day, the brother next to him in age said, "Hey, where d'you go when you're missing?"

"None of your business," replied Peter. "Secret, see."

"Aw, go on, show me. Won't tell anyone, promise."

"No, now shut up."

"Stupid anyway, to have a place just to yourself. Daft. At your age. You're eleven, not a baby."

"You wouldn't think that if you saw it. It's great there. Peaceful."

"If it's so great, then show it to me. Don't be selfish."

And Peter thought. Should he take his brother to it, prove to him that it wasn't daft? Or perhaps... it was daft.

Now think:

Is it daft to want to be alone sometimes – as long as an adult knows where you are? Do we need to get away from noise and interruptions at times? And should Peter take his brother to his special place?

(You could discuss this or pass on to the main story.)

THE STORY

Our true story today begins in a quiet place that's very special.

The old man lowered himself on to the little garden seat. He loved it here in this little corner, away from all the busy-ness of his life, surrounded by the beauty of an English garden. But this English garden was thousands of miles from England. It was in India.

Suddenly there was a rustling by his feet. A tiny lizard had appeared from under the bluebell patch to find out whether this giant, who'd already disturbed his lazy afternoon, was going to ruin it completely.

But the old man, whose name was William Carey, had not come to make noise. He'd come here, as he did so often, to be quiet, to pray – and to think back over his life. What a life it had been!

He'd been born in 1761 and grew up in Paulerspury in Northamptonshire. Even as a boy he loved nature, and collected a marvellous little zoo of insects. His bedroom was like a mini Natural History Museum. And what he couldn't collect, he'd climb – he was only a little lad, but he'd get up a tree in no time if it would give him a better view of a bird perched there.

At fourteen he was apprenticed to a shoemaker, and he became a good one. Even though he had to walk from village to village to deliver the shoes he'd made, he still had some spare time. And William, as you'll see, hated spare time. So he took on a second job – teaching in the village school.

He loved teaching geography. He made a special globe. Perhaps you can guess what he made it from – leather, with different coloured leathers for the different countries. And as he used that globe, he kept on being reminded of lands where the people knew nothing of God's love.

But he still had some free time. So he learnt some languages – Latin and Greek... and Hebrew... and Italian... and Dutch... and French. On top of all this, he became a preacher, walking up to twelve miles to deliver his Sunday sermon.

Eventually he could stand it no longer. He just had to go to one of those countries on his globe and tell the people about God's love. But where? As he prayed, he knew. India.

His wife though was not in love with the idea. It was so far away and, besides, she was expecting another child. William tried to persuade her but in the end it was decided that he would go out first with their oldest son, Felix, aged eight, and the rest of the family would follow when William had made a home.

It took a long time to find a ship willing to take them as passengers. But finally they did and William and Felix said their sad goodbyes and travelled to the port. But just before sailing time, the captain changed his mind – he wouldn't take them.

So they had to go home again. You can imagine William saying to God, "Lord, you're bigger than that captain. Why did you allow him to change his mind?"

By the time they got home the baby had been born – and his wife had been so miserable without her husband and oldest son that she said, "All right, I'll come. We'll all come." William was thrilled. He understood now why God had allowed the delay.

And, amazingly, they found a ship to take the whole family almost straight away. They waved goodbye to England on June 13th, 1793.

The lizard was still standing there gazing up as if to say, "What are you thinking about, giant?"

And William would have said, "I'm thinking about how God never lets us down. He always works things out in the end."

After five months they arrived in Calcutta and William was offered a job managing a factory. He quickly got down to learning the local language, Bengali, not just so he could talk to the workers, but also to translate the Bible. He longed for the people to be able to read all the stories which had thrilled him since childhood.

It was a tough language to learn – it used a different alphabet, and there were no dictionaries or text books to help him. Finally he did it. Now the translation. But how to get it printed?

The time had come for a move, to a town called Serampore, where, with other missionary families, he bought a large house with plenty of room to set up printing presses. Pages of Matthew and Mark and so on were soon rolling off them.

For William, Bengali was just the beginning. Soon he'd begun learning another Indian language, doing another translation, then another language, and so on. And in his spare time, he created that beautiful garden, using seeds and bulbs sent from England.

Then, suddenly – "Fire! Fire! The printing room's on fire!" A tower of flame blazed against the night sky. The printing presses were rescued, but the work of many months was destroyed.

In his sadness, William went to his special place in the garden and prayed. And he remembered the delayed voyage. Could something good come out of something bad again? He knew it could. And it did. William did the translation work a second time, and it was a much better translation than before. Yes – God had worked it out for the best.

But he still had a bit of spare time – so he took on two more jobs – church minister and college lecturer. Phew!

The lizard, satisfied that the giant meant no harm, scuttled back under the bluebells to sleep. But it wasn't time for William to sleep yet.

"Thank you, God, for these few minutes of quiet," he prayed. "Thank you for reminding me of your faithfulness."

And as the sun dipped down behind the mahogany tree, he made his way back to work.

I think you'll agree that William Carey did not like wasting time. In fact, within six months of arriving at Serampore, he'd put 427 types of plant in his garden. And by the time he died on June 9th, 1834, he'd translated the Bible, or part of it, into 35 languages and dialects.

He was perhaps one of the busiest men who ever lived. But the busier he got, the more he valued his special, quiet place.

TIME OF REFLECTION

Anywhere can be a special, quiet place – a garden, a bedroom, the cupboard under the stairs. Let's make this (room, hall...) a special place for a moment and sit quietly and think about what's important to us – perhaps to think about God's love as William Carey did, or to think, or pray, about a problem. Or just to appreciate all we have. A moment of total quiet then...

BIBLE BITS

Jesus liked to take time to be quiet. After the feeding of the five thousand the Bible says,

"After sending the people away, he went up a hill by himself to pray."

(Matthew 14:23)

Another time, "Very early the next morning, long before daylight, Jesus got up and ... went ... to a lonely place where he prayed."

(Mark 1:35)

PRAYER

Help us, Lord, not to waste time. But help us too not to spend all our time rushing about. Help us sometimes to be still and quiet, to think, to appreciate and to pray, as William Carey did, as you did, Lord Jesus. Amen

VARIATIONS ON A THEME

Children write very well about special places. A selection of their pieces, on either real or imagined places, could be incorporated into the assembly.

Or: you could write a little Bengali on acetate to show how difficult it would have been for Carey to learn. If you have any Bengali-speaking pupils, that would be ideal (or Hindi, or Punjabi, or Gujerati – Carey translated those too!).

QUIZ QUESTIONS

1. What was William Carey's first job?
2. Then he took another job as well – what was it?
3. What did he use to make the classroom globe?
4. What kept coming into his mind as he used it?
5. What caused the delay in William leaving England?
6. What good came out of the delay?
7. How old was Felix when he left England?
8. Give one reason why it would have been hard to learn Bengali.
9. What good came out of the fire?
10. How many languages and dialects did he learn?

CORRIE TEN BOOM

Forgiving those who hurt me – WW2 prison camp

Other themes: fear, prayer, the Bible, heaven

THE PROBLEM

Listen to this and think what you'd do if you were in Emma's situation.

It was the first day of secondary school – but already Emma knew she was going to like it. Her parents had asked if she could be put in the same group as her two best friends. And it had worked out. She'd met up with them outside the school a few minutes before and they'd been directed to a classroom to wait for their group tutor.

The last year in the old school had been a miserable one for Emma, and all because of Lisa Jo, who'd bullied her – she'd poked fun at her, got her into trouble, it had just gone on and on. Emma's only friends had been in another class. But now it would be OK.

Late ones were still coming in. Suddenly Emma felt a shudder run through her. Lisa Jo had entered the room. She looked different though – lonely, unsure, gone were the swagger and the smirks.

She came right up to Emma whose heart had begun thumping.

"Looks like we're together again," Lisa Jo said. "Look, Emma, we didn't get on last year, but what about making up, being friends from now on?"

Emma's fear turned to anger. Friends? With Lisa Jo? No way. She hadn't even said sorry, she only wanted to be friends because she'd been split from her old mates. So – just forgive and forget? As if last year never happened? No way!

Now think:
Is Emma right or wrong to think this way? What would you do in her situation?

(You could discuss this or pass on to the main story.)

THE STORY

Now here's a true story.

When the guards slid open the door, Corrie Ten Boom could see only darkness inside. Outside was bright sunlight. In there it was as dark as death.

"Quick! Get in! In!" one of the guards yelled.

Corrie and the other women hauled themselves up into the darkness. There was no choice – the guards had guns. It was the carriage of a goods train, but now it was being used to transport people. In seconds the carriage was so full that Corrie was pushed up against the back wall. Many of the women were crying, some were screaming. How glad Corrie was to have her sister Betsie with her. And how glad she was that God was with her. She was not afraid, not deep down. For what was the worst thing these German soldiers could do to her? Kill her? But then she would be with Jesus for ever.

There were eighty women in the carriage now. They were just able to sit down with their legs wrapped round the person in front. It grew unbearably hot. The train began moving but it didn't help much.

As Corrie stroked her sister's feverish forehead, she thought back through the last years, back to when the German army had invaded their country, Holland, soon after the start of World War 2. It was a terrible time for everyone, but the Jewish people suffered the most. Corrie saw them being pushed into trucks to be taken to the prison camps.

As they prayed for them, Corrie's family had the idea of building a secret room in their house where Jewish people could hide from the patrols until an escape route could be found for them. But someone betrayed them and the family was arrested, to be taken to Germany. Corrie and Betsie had been able to stick together, but they didn't know how long they would be allowed to live.

On the fourth day the train clanked to a halt.

"Out! Get out!" shouted the guards. "You walk now!"

The women were so weak but what choice was there? Finally they saw their destination: Ravensbruck prison camp. As Corrie and Betsie entered the massive gates, they knew there was almost no chance of coming out alive.

All the women were taken to the shower room. Corrie's heart started thumping when she saw that everyone had to undress in front of the guards. For under her dress she had hidden her precious Bible and some medicine for Betsie. They'd be discovered and taken away! No, it mustn't happen!

"Dear God, please... " she murmured.

Just then Betsie, even sicker now, needed to be taken to the toilet. "Use the drains in the shower room," said the guard harshly. The sisters moved ahead of the queue of women undressing and went in.

"Dear God, please..."

Yes! There in the corner was a pile of old benches. She could hide the Bible and medicine behind them, together with Betsie's warm sweater.

Later, after their shower, Corrie slipped over to the benches and pushed the things under the prison dress she'd been given. "Thank you, God, thank you," she prayed.

But – wait – what was this? A guard was searching the women on the way out of the shower room. Corrie prayed again – she knew that the God who had answered one prayer could answer another. She stood in the line. She came nearer and nearer to the guard. The bulge under the thin prison dress was so obvious.

Now the woman ahead of Corrie was being searched. She was searched three times before being allowed to move off.

Then something strange happened. The guard didn't seem to notice Corrie. He went straight to Betsie, next in line.

There was another search as they left the building. Same thing. The guard came to Corrie, but instead of searching her, just told her to hurry up, and then pushed her out – with her precious possessions undiscovered.

That Bible was certainly well used. Corrie would hold services in their dormitory, Barracks 28 – with softly sung hymns, whispered prayers and Bible verses telling of God's comfort and love.

More and more women came to the services. Corrie knew if a guard came in, the Bible would be taken, and they would all be punished. But no guard came near. Only later did she find out why. Barracks 28 was famous amongst the guards for its fleas, and the guards did not want their smart uniforms crawling with fleas. Corrie reckoned each flea was a tiny miracle from God.

Long hours of heavy work and very little food weakened Corrie and Betsie, and pain, cruelty and death were all around them. But they could see beyond these things to heaven – a place of no pain or sadness, waiting for them.

And one day Betsie died. Her face was full of peace and happiness.

Two days later, Corrie was ordered to go to the prison office. She feared they'd found out about the Bible. But she was just handed a piece of paper. It said: "Released". She was free.

But – how... why... ?

She found out later it had been a mistake. But she was well away by then.

A week after Corrie's release all the women in the camp of Corrie's age were killed.

When the war was over, Corrie asked God, "What do you want me to do?"

And she knew that she should open homes for those who had survived the prison camps. And she should travel, all over the world, telling how she had known God's help and love even in Ravensbruck.

One evening, in a church in Germany, after she had spoken, a man came up to her wanting to shake hands. Many people did of course, nothing unusual in that. But then her blood turned cold. For she recognised the man. He was the guard at the shower room door in Ravensbruck. And she remembered his cruelty, his total lack of pity. It was because of him, and the many like him, that millions had suffered and died.

"I am a Christian now," he said. "God has forgiven me."

Corrie's thoughts screamed out, But I cannot forgive. I will not forgive. And then she thought of Jesus. Jesus, who'd been nailed to a cross and who'd prayed for his executioners, "Father, forgive them."

"Jesus," Corrie whispered in her heart, "give me your forgiveness for this man."

And Jesus did. She was able to take the man's hand and forgive him from her heart. Just as Jesus forgave.

She went on spreading the message of forgiveness and love until she died, in 1983, on her 91st birthday.

TIME OF REFLECTION

Think now: are you holding a grudge against someone, unwilling to forgive them? Is the wrong they've done greater than what those camp guards did to Corrie? Is it greater than what those Roman soldiers did to Jesus? Yet they forgave.

Just take a moment to think about this.

BIBLE BITS

This is what the Bible says:

"Love your enemies and pray for those who persecute you."
(Matthew 5:44)

"You must forgive one another just as the Lord has forgiven you." (Colossians 3:13)

(Jesus's words to Peter about forgiving again and again – Matthew 18:21,22 – are appropriate too.)

PRAYER

Father, help us to be ready to forgive, never to hold on to a grudge. This won't be easy. Like Corrie, we need your help. Amen

VARIATION ON A THEME

The pupils could be reminded of the section of Joseph's story which shows his forgiveness for the brothers who had put him in a pit and sold him into slavery (Genesis chapters 37 and 45).

GORDON WILSON

Forgiving those who take away what I love – peacemaking in N. Ireland

Other themes: death, God's comfort

THE PROBLEM

Listen carefully to this story and think what you'd do.

It was the best thing he'd ever done – everyone said so. Even Mr James, the art teacher, who was hard to impress, said: "Martin, this is just terrific." All this praise was a bit new for Martin – he wasn't very good at school work generally – but it made all the hours of hard work worth it.

Perhaps it was Martin's love of the sport that had enabled him to do it so well – but this little clay figure of a footballer dribbling a ball up the field was perfect, no denying it. Even the Man United colours had come out just right after the varnishing and firing.

Now it had pride of place in the craft display for open day. The next day! – Martin was excited.

When he arrived at school the following morning, the whole place was in uproar. He overheard two teachers talking. "They got in through the craft room. Damaged everything they could get their hands on. The police are on their way."

Then he saw Mr James coming towards him, his hands cupped round something he was carrying. Martin's heart began thumping hard.

Mr James opened his hands. There was the little clay figure. Shattered. Impossible to mend.

Martin began to cry, his whole body shaking.

"You could make another one," said Mr James softly.

Martin stopped sobbing and shouted, "What's the point? I'm not bothering again. Ever." And he grabbed the pieces from the teacher's hands, threw them on the ground and stormed off.

Now think:

What would you say to Martin if you were his friend? Would you say, "Never mind, it was only a model"? Would that help? What about, "When we know who did it, we'll go and break their stuff"? Is that any better?

(You could discuss this or pass on to the main story.)

THE STORY

(Don't rush the reading of this.)

Listen now to the true story of someone who lost much, much more than a clay model.

The eighth of November 1987, Enniskillen, Northern Ireland.

Remembrance Day.

The father and daughter stood close together for the open air service at the War Memorial, for it was cold and windy. But the weather hadn't put them off coming. They both wanted to pay their respects to those who had died, not just in the wars, but in the more recent troubles in their own land. There'd been so much bloodshed, so much suffering.

The father, Gordon Wilson, a shopkeeper in the town, knew there was no easy solution to the differences between Catholics and Protestants, but why, oh why, did innocent people have to die? Bombs in buildings, bombs in cars, you never knew where the terrorists would plant one next. And what for?

He looked round. He hoped the police had searched the area properly. But no, surely at a service honouring the dead, surely they would have the decency not to strike here.

He always stood in this spot for the service, by the wall of an old building. He was pleased his youngest daughter Marie could be with him this year. She was twenty, a nurse at a hospital in Belfast, home for the weekend. He was so proud of her, so proud.

Then it happened. The world seemed to explode around them. The wall shuddered, then fell on top of them. The unthinkable had come true. The provisional IRA had planted a bomb, just by where they were standing. Gordon was thrown forward, then felt a pounding on his back as the rubble piled on top of him.

He was aware of screaming all around him, but he could do nothing about it. Then he felt a hand coming through the rubble, grabbing his. Marie's hand. They were together and they were alive. He heard her shout out that she loved him before her hand seemed to lose its grip.

Father and daughter were pulled out from under the broken wall and rushed to hospital. Gordon had injured his shoulder. But Marie's injuries were far worse, and later that day, she died.

The family members – Gordon, his wife Joan, and two other children – comforted each other, gave each other strength to go on. But they were aware of someone else comforting them too, someone with his arms wrapped right round them. God was there, suffering with them.

Catholics and Protestants were able to come together and comfort the families of the eleven people who had died in the blast. They knew that true Christians, whatever church they went to, hated the violence, and were sad that people might blame God for it.

But Gordon didn't blame God – he knew that God is love. And he didn't need to take revenge either, for he knew that God himself would judge the terrorists in his own time. And he believed he would see Marie again in heaven.

Over the next days Gordon was interviewed on radio and TV. People were astonished at his lack of hatred and bitterness.

More and more invitations to speak poured in, not only from Ireland, but from other countries too. People listened who had lost loved ones, who were finding it difficult to go on, who felt God had forsaken them, who were full of bitterness. And Gordon, this shopkeeper from a little town, showed them they could go on, that God had not forsaken them and never would, and that being bitter wouldn't help. He brought them comfort and hope.

But he wanted to do more. He wanted to help bring peace to his country. He accepted an invitation to join the Irish parliament so he could plead with the country's leaders for a united, peaceful Ireland.

Little by little things did change. As Gordon and others spoke, people began to see they had to put the hurts and hatred of the past behind them and think about the future. And eventually, on Good Friday 1998, a peace treaty was signed.

But Gordon Wilson was not there to see it. He had died peacefully three years before.

After his death people from all over the world wrote to his widow saying how much Gordon had meant to them. He had not just told them the best way to cope with loss, but shown them as well. God had helped him, and he had passed on that help to others.

So Marie's death had not been in vain.

TIME OF REFLECTION

Life is not always easy. When something bad happens it can really hurt. But later on these bad times make it possible for us to help someone else, to say to that person, "I know what you're feeling." And that can really help.

Is there anyone you know who's hurting today? Can you do anything to help?

Just take a moment to think about this.

BIBLE BITS

David in the Bible knew God's comfort:

"The Lord is my shepherd...
Even if I go through the deepest darkness,
I will not be afraid, Lord, for you are with me.
I know that your goodness and love will be with me all my life."
(Psalm 23)

But the apostle Paul knew that he should pass that comfort on:

"He helps us in all our troubles, so that we are able to help others who have all kinds of troubles."
(2 Corinthians 1:4)

PRAYER

Lord, you know what it's like to feel hurt inside. You had really bad things happen to you. So you understand, even if no one else does. Thank you that you never turn away. Help us to accept your comfort and then be ready to comfort others. Amen

VARIATIONS ON A THEME

The most valuable addition here would be to think in more detail about what Jesus did suffer (betrayal, desertion by friends, mocking, physical pain) and how he always reacted in love. Every bad feeling children have, Jesus has been there. They need to see that he understands.

If the atmosphere is not right for this, then children could read their own stories (fictional or true) about a friend being there at a bad time.

JOHN PATON

Forgiving those who make my life difficult – missionary work in the Pacific

Other themes: courage, endurance

THE PROBLEM

Listen to this and see what you think.

"Aw, please, Lizzie, just for a minute. Please."

"No."

Shelley leaned across the table even further. "But I need it. Please."

"Last time you borrowed a pen, you broke it."

"Yeah, I know, but I said sorry *and* I replaced it. Cost me a week's pocket money."

"And look what happened to that book of mine last week."

"Sorry. Just couldn't stop my baby brother scribbling on it. I tried to rub it out but – "

The teacher's voice cut in. "Lizzie, Shelley, get on please. I've asked you before."

Lizzie sighed. She was fed up with Shelley. She'd asked for a move, but the teacher said it wasn't possible. One day she'd blow up at her, she knew it.

Shelley was whispering now. Well, what passed for a whisper with her. "Anyway, you said you'd forgiven me for all that."

"But I have to keep on forgiving you, don't I? It never stops."

"Yeah, I know I'm clumsy and I've never got the right stuff, but – "

"No. Now shut up."

"Aw, Lizzie, just for a minute. Please."

Now think:

Should she lose her temper with Shelley? Should she just ignore her? Or should she forget the past and lend her the pen?

(You could discuss this or pass on to the main story.)

THE STORY

But the aggravations Lizzie suffered were nothing compared with what the person in today's true story went through. It happened about 150 years ago.

The man came running out of the jungle to the missionary's house. He was breathless.

"Please – I need your help! I need to talk!"

John Paton was in the garden hanging out his sheets and blankets to air. He had been a missionary on the island for long enough to know this man all too well. This was Miaki, the war chief who had been against John and his work from the start. What was he up to now?

Miaki darted inside the house and John followed. Miaki began umming and aaring, he didn't seem to know how to begin his story.

Suddenly there was a cry from a lady working in the garden. "Come quickly, they're stealing the bedclothes!"

Miaki raced out of the house, shouting, "I'll get them back for you!"

But John knew the bedclothes had probably gone for good. It had all been one of Miaki's tricks.

It had been like this ever since John had come to Tanna, one of the islands of the New Hebrides, east of Australia. He looked round his house thoughtfully. Oh well, one good thing, there wasn't much left to steal now.

They were clever thieves on Tanna. Invite them in and something would go. They couldn't hide it in their pockets for they didn't wear clothes, so they hid it in their long plaits of hair, or in an armpit, or they would knock something small on the floor, then curl their big toe round it and walk out with it hidden under their foot. If what they wanted was too large for that, they might even just pick it up and stroll out.

So why didn't John demand things back, threaten them with the law? Well, for a start, there was no law, and for another, you're careful what you say to cannibals. John had not come all this way to be eaten.

And he had come a long way – from near Dumfries in Scotland. He'd come because people were needed to tell the islanders about a God of love.

For love was in short supply on Tanna. When the men weren't waving their tomahawks at each other, they were savagely beating the women to get them to work harder. Children were uncared for, and old people were often allowed to starve, or killed more quickly if they were in the way.

So did he regret coming? No. The problems made him long all the more that they come to know Jesus. He would go to their villages and explain what God was like, what he had done for them. They were very impressed – yes, this was a great God, but, oh no, they could not turn from their other gods, they would get jealous and might do terrible things.

So John prayed and waited.

One day some natives came up to the house screaming in terror. "Help us! There is something coming through the sea, pouring out smoke!"

John realised what this "monster" was – a British steamship. The Captain must have heard there was a British subject on the island and decided to make a friendly visit. The natives had never seen such a vessel.

"Ah," said John. "This is a mighty ship sent by Queen Victoria. I will have to give a report on your behaviour, I'm afraid... "

Now the fear went up a notch.

"I must tell them the truth about your stealing... "

"Oh, no, no! Please – everything will be returned. Please!"

"But, look, the ship is coming into harbour now."

The natives had never run so fast. A huge pile of John's pots and pans, blankets and knives, all kinds of stuff, began growing on his doorstep.

"Where," John asked as he surveyed it all, "is the lid of the kettle?"

The natives gazed at each other in horror. "Oh no, it's on the other side of the island. But tomorrow you will have it. Please!"

John eventually agreed, enjoying every second of their panic. But he knew as soon as the ship had disappeared over the horizon, his belongings would start disappearing again too.

In all his troubles he remembered Jesus, how *he* had suffered much more. John had been deceived by strangers, but Jesus had been betrayed by a friend, which was surely worse. John had lost many possessions, but Jesus had given up everything. John had been near death many times, but Jesus had actually died, and in a terrible way.

But *he* had not given up. So John would not give up either. He, like Jesus, would go on forgiving, go on praying, go on seeking to do good.

He had at least one friend on Tanna – Clutha, his faithful and fierce bodyguard, a little dog actually, a retriever. If anyone tried to get in the house at night, Clutha would bark, then begin pulling at the bedclothes. If someone came at John with a club, he would jump up at them like an uncoiled spring and frighten them half to death. The natives had more fear of the mighty warrior Clutha than they had of John!

One day though there came a situation even Clutha could do nothing about. John was working in his garden when he realised he was being surrounded by a large circle of natives, including the dreadful Miaki. They took their positions, then stood totally still and quiet, each one holding a rifle – pointed straight at John! There was no way of escape. He was frightened, so he began to pray – hard. And he felt an incredible sense of peace. God was in charge. It would be all right. So he got on with his gardening. And little by little the natives disappeared back into the jungle. They were powerless to shoot. God had not allowed it.

John worked on two islands, Tanna and Aniwa. And it was on Aniwa he saw things happen. One of the chiefs really latched on to what John was saying and became a Christian. This seemed to give permission to his tribe to consider it for themselves and some of them said yes to Jesus too.

Today there are many Christians on the New Hebrides – or Vanuatu as the islands are now known. In fact the national motto is, "In God We Stand". Caring has replaced cannibalism – and their big toes remain straight at all times!

It was because people who loved God, like John Paton, not only went, but *stayed*.

TIME OF REFLECTION

Now, think of the things that make you feel fed up, that you find hard to put up with. God asks of us the same things he asked of John – whatever happens, go on forgiving, go on being kind and generous. God can help us do this. And think not only of what John put up with, but what Jesus put up with too.

Just take a moment to think about this.

BIBLE BITS

"Then Peter came to Jesus and asked, 'Lord, if my brother keeps on sinning against me, how many times do I have to forgive him? Seven times?'
'No, not seven times,' answered Jesus, 'but seventy times seven.'"

(Matthew 18:21–22)

In other words, don't count how often you forgive someone, just go on doing it!

"Love is patient and kind; ... love does not keep a record of wrongs; ...
Love never gives up."

(I Corinthians 13:4,5,7)

PRAYER

Jesus, thank you that you do not give up on us. Please give us your patience and your forgiving attitude, both at home and at school. Help us not to get all steamed up, but to go on caring, go on sharing. Amen

VARIATION ON A THEME

Look more at some of the potential aggravations – and worse – in Jesus' life and how he reacted. Pupils could dramatise and act out a couple of the following – perhaps, before each one, acting out what Jesus did not do – got impatient, lost his temper, hit back, etc:

Interruptions: Mark 6:30–34
Mockery: Luke 8:52–55
      Luke 22:63–65; 23:34
Betrayal: Matthew 26:47–50

QUIZ QUESTIONS
1. Where are the New Hebrides?
2. Where did John come from?
3. When his possessions were stolen, why didn't he go to the police?
4. Why were the natives afraid of the steamship?
5. What was missing from the pile of returned goods?
6. Tell me one way Jesus suffered more than John.
7. Another.
8. Tell me one way Clutha would defend John.
9. Another.
10. What is the national motto of the islands today?

JOHN NEWTON

Saying sorry may not be enough – slave trading in Africa

Other themes: repentance, stealing

THE PROBLEM

Listen to this and think which of the two characters is right.

They knew the cloakroom thief would be caught in the end. But it was still a surprise when it happened. The news got round the school playground as fast as Concorde in a hurry. "Have you heard? It was Zelda. They caught her red-handed."

Caught, in fact, with her hand in someone's coat pocket just that breaktime. Mrs Masters had forgotten something from her classroom, hurried back down the corridor, and there she was.

And now she was sitting with Mrs Masters, sobbing away.

"Yeah, it was me, every time," she spluttered. "I did it once, didn't get caught, so I did it again, and again, couldn't seem to stop. But I'm sorry now. I really am."

Mrs Masters passed her another tissue.

"Yes, Zelda, I believe you are sorry. You got carried away. But it's not enough just to – "

"I know, Miss," Zelda burst in. "I'll go round saying sorry to everyone I stole from, I promise."

"That's good, Zelda, but I meant we need to think about how you are going to pay the money back."

Zelda's wide eyes looked up at Mrs Masters from above the tissue. "Pay it back, Miss?" She looked horrified. "Oh, but I can't do that. I spent it all on CDs. Aw, that's not fair."

Now think:
Who's right? Is it enough just for Zelda to say sorry, or should she also pay back what she stole?

(You could discuss this or pass on to the main story.)

THE STORY

Now let me take you back about two centuries for our true story.

She stood on the deck of the slave ship, her black skin shivering despite the heat of the African sun. There was panic in her eyes as she stared around her. She noticed a young white man leaning on the side of the ship, gazing at her, grinning. With desperation in her voice she began shouting out to him in her native language. She could have been begging to be allowed to go home, or pleading to know where her baby was – he had been snatched from her arms when the slave traders captured her near her village – or simply crying out for mercy.

But the man didn't know and he certainly didn't care. For he was John Newton, not one for showing pity. Not a nice man at all, in fact. He'd been in the Royal Navy for a time, despising those above him in rank, and bullying those below. He was foul-mouthed and foul-tempered, and loved to mock the Bible and those who believed in it. But he hadn't liked the discipline of the Navy, so now he'd joined the crew of a British slave ship. It offered him adventure, a good living, and, above all, the freedom to act as badly as he liked.

Suddenly the girl felt her arms grabbed from behind, saw the branding iron getting closer and closer to her bare flesh. She screamed. But John Newton had lost interest and turned away. To him the slave girl was not a human being, but just goods to be bought and sold. He did not turn back as she was taken sobbing to be chained in the stinking hold. Instead he gazed out at the great Atlantic Ocean. Soon the ship would be crossing it to sell the slaves in the West Indies. John breathed in the salty air. What a life! He was nineteen and felt like the king of the seas.

Until the storm.

His ship, the *Greyhound*, was on the way home. John was asleep in his bunk. Warm and secure. Suddenly the world seemed to shatter around him. A massive wave had crashed down on the ship and the icy water was gushing into his cabin.

Then another wave smashed down. And another.

John had to fight against the rush of water to get up to the deck. "Man the pumps!" someone shouted at him. "It's our only chance!"

It was exhausting and it seemed hopeless. John would look up and see a mountain of black water towering over him, then the ship would be thrown as if by some giant hand to the top of that mountain, only to slide headlong into the next valley. The ship could not hold together in this.

And John understood – he was about to die.

And he felt terribly, terribly afraid. Of what might come... afterwards. For what if... what if he was wrong in what he believed? No, please, no, his thoughts screamed. It can't be. There can't be a God waiting to judge me... can there? And the Bible that I've mocked for so long – it's not true... is it?

He had to know. Between turns at the pumps he found a New Testament and read. His eyes swept the pages frantically. Please, please, don't be true! He read in terror, on and on.

The storm stopped. The ship drifted in the stillness. But John still read on, his panic turning little by little to peace. By the time the *Greyhound* limped into Ireland weeks later he knew not only that the Bible was true, but that God need not be a God of judgment but of forgiveness – a forgiveness which John accepted eagerly.

Much later he wrote a hymn about this experience, 'Amazing Grace', which – amazingly – was to top the British charts almost two hundred years later, in 1972.

Strange as it seems, although he was now a Christian, he continued in the slave trade. He even became captain of a slave ship. He simply could not see the slaves as people, created by God, loved by God, just like him.

But over the next years he began to realise he was wrong. At first he thought it would be enough just to treat the slaves better, but then he realised that God wanted him to stop slave-trading altogether.

So he became a minister in the Church of England, first in Buckinghamshire, then in London, and, as you know, a hymn writer.

But still God's voice kept whispering – something more needs to be done, something more.

And finally, John understood. He began to see the slave trade through God's eyes, saw the full horror of it, and felt deep shame that he had been involved in it. But what could he do to make up? He felt sorry, and he could say sorry – but what good would that do to the hundreds of people he had harmed? What did God want him to do?

And he realised, no, he could not change the past, but he could change the future.

He got busy. He persuaded his old friend, the MP William Wilberforce, to make the injustice of slavery known to the Prime Minister and other influential people. And he wrote a booklet. "I know these appalling things are true," he wrote, "for I did them."

Nothing happened. So he kept at it. All through his old age he kept badgering people: "Slave trading must stop."

And eventually, in 1807, a law saying just that was passed.

John Newton also helped to start no less than three missionary societies to go to that same part of Africa to show God's love.

I wonder if the missionaries came to the village of the girl at the beginning of the story. If so, the villagers would have understood that John Newton hadn't just said he was sorry, he'd proved it.

TIME OF REFLECTION

Let's think: is there anyone you've done something wrong to and although you've said sorry – at least I hope you have – you need to do something more? For example, if you were rude, to show you respect that person; if you bullied, to show special kindness; if you broke something of theirs, to replace it. To *prove* you're sorry.

Just take a moment to consider if you need to do this.

BIBLE BITS

John the Baptist knew that words were not enough. He told people:

"Do those things that will show that you have turned from your sins."

(Luke 3:8)

(Also the story of Zacchaeus – see VARIATIONS below.)

PRAYER

Lord, it's easy to hurt people and it's almost as easy to say sorry. But it's not so easy to show we mean it. That costs. Help us to see that sometimes saying sorry and feeling sorry are not enough. Amen

VARIATIONS ON A THEME

If you have a short extrovert amongst your pupils then the story of Zacchaeus is fun to act out, perhaps flamboyantly mimed while you read Luke 19:1–10. The idea of proving you're sorry comes out clearly in verse 8. It would probably fit best after the TIME OF REFLECTION: "Here's one character who knew what he needed to do... "

And, of course, if you can find the chart-topping version of 'Amazing Grace' (by the Royal Scots Dragoon Guards Band) in the depths of your record collection, great. You may wish to read, even explain, the words.

QUIZ QUESTIONS

1. Why did John Newton prefer the slave ship to the Navy?
2. How old was he when he joined the slave ship?
3. Name the ship which nearly sank.
4. Why was John so afraid when the storm came?
5. Name the hymn he wrote about his experience.
6. How come he continued in the slave trade as a Christian?
7. He was a church minister first in – ?
8. Then in – ?
9. When he saw how wrong he was, he wrote a booklet. How would readers know he was not exaggerating?
10. What did William Wilberforce do?

WHY HAVE A QUIZ?

So why have I given over so much space to quiz questions?

1. If children know a quiz is coming they will listen very attentively.
2. The quiz becomes a form of revision, helping them remember the story.
3. It tests, not just memory of the facts, but also understanding of what the assembly has tried to put across.
4. Children enjoy a quiz, and that's important.

The questions here can be used immediately after the assembly or by individual teachers later in the day.

There are many possible formats for quizzes. The one I like best is a version of noughts and crosses:

∫　Draw a simple four line grid on acetate or on the board and the numbers 1–9 beside it

∫　Draw the same grid on a private slip of paper or next to the questions, and fill it with the numbers, e.g.

```
4  6  2
1  9  5
8  3  7
```

Don't show this to the pupils!

∫　Divide the pupils into two teams, and ask a question to the first team. But instead of the team member choosing a box, he chooses a number, say 8.

∫　Cross off 8 on the list and say, "And number 8 is... in a corner! Well done!" So a big X goes in that corner on the blank grid.

∫　Team two gets a question and so on, until one team has a line.

This maintains much more suspense than the normal version, where the team which goes first, if they know how to play and get the questions right, will always win.

Four (or Three) in a Row – played on a large grid – also works well. And there's always Snakes and Ladders, fun when played with a huge foam dice.

But remember you only have ten questions. You could make more of your own or use questions from the story used previously, but a quiz is best when it's short and snappy. You may wish to juggle the assembly order to finish on a quieter note.

SUBJECTLINK INDEX

The numbers pertain to the chapters as listed at the front of the book.